THE LIVING WORD
OF ST JOHN

Some more books of White Eagle's teaching

THE GENTLE BROTHER
GOLDEN HARVEST
HEAL THYSELF
JESUS, TEACHER AND HEALER
MORNING LIGHT
THE PATH OF THE SOUL
PRAYER IN THE NEW AGE
THE QUIET MIND
SPIRITUAL UNFOLDMENT 1
SPIRITUAL UNFOLDMENT 2
SPIRITUAL UNFOLDMENT 3
SPIRITUAL UNFOLDMENT 4
THE STILL VOICE
SUNRISE
THE WAY OF THE SUN
WISDOM FROM WHITE EAGLE

The Living Word of St John

White Eagle's interpretation of the gospel

THE WHITE EAGLE PUBLISHING TRUST
LISS · HAMPSHIRE · ENGLAND

THE LIVING WORD *first published December 1949*
This edition, substantially
revised and with much new matter, published for the
first time as THE LIVING WORD OF ST JOHN, *September 1979*
Fifth impression June 1990

British Library Cataloguing in Publication Data

Cooke, Grace
The living word of St John – 2nd ed.
1. Spirit writings
I. Title   II. White Eagle   III. Living word
133.9'3   BF1301

ISBN 0–85487–044–X

SET IN 12 ON 14 PT MONOPHOTO EHRHARDT
PRINTED AND BOUND IN GREAT BRITAIN BY
WILLIAM CLOWES LTD, BECCLES AND LONDON

CONTENTS

Note to the 1979 edition

A major part of the cost of printing this book was donated by American members of the White Eagle Lodge in 1976, the year of the bicentenary of the American Declaration of Independence. The White Eagle Publishing Trust is grateful for this generous gift.

PREFACE

THE LIVING WORD, first published in December 1949 and out of print since 1965, is probably the most asked-for of all those early books of White Eagle's teaching, and we have always promised ourselves that it would be reprinted in the fulness of time. The talks of which it is the substance, based upon the gospel of St John, were given by White Eagle through the instrumentality of Mrs Grace Cooke between January 1943 and July 1945. It might be thought that wartime London would not be the most likely background for a sustained message from the world of spirit of such deep love and wisdom and mystical truth, yet perhaps it was the very contrast and the need of the hour which brought forth the profound truths to be found in these pages.

There must still be those who can recall coming out of the blackout and the fear into the quiet sanctuary where peace enfolded them and all was well. They will remember the stillness, the expectancy, and will recall the gentle loving voice which yet spoke with such authority, and above all they will remember being raised out of conflict and suffering by the power of the message; and the miracle of unfolding vision and ever-deepening understanding it brought.

Readers may well ask why such an important message has been allowed to remain out of print for so long. It was a big undertaking. Over the years much has come to us from White Eagle to amplify and clarify themes touched upon then; he has built upon that early teaching, and it was felt that a new edition of the book should where possible incorporate such teaching. This of course has required research. There has also been some rearrangement for the sake of clarity. For instance, in the original, chapter two of the gospel served as an introduction, but it is now in its proper chronological place. The answers in the 'Question and Answer' section of the original, where the questions were relevant, have been incorporated into the main text – again for clarity's sake. The same applies to the substance of the 'Afterword'. Where later teaching by White Eagle could not be incorporated into the text without interrupting the flow of thought it has been included in an appendix.

Working on the manuscript has been a labour of love; as chapter after chapter unfolded one became utterly uplifted by the sublime over-all theme which built up, of the redemptive power of the Christ spirit through the everyday life of man. The unseen often seemed very close and there was one particular day when the gospel suddenly became almost unbearably alive and immediate. It was no longer a question of looking back to happenings of two thousand years ago and words of men long dead; the words became alive and the whole story was in the present, as seen and felt through the eyes and heart of the 'disciple whom Jesus loved'. Both were so real and human and loving of mankind today. It was an experience impossible to express adequately in words, but the memory will be with me always.

There is some connection, I think, between this experience and another, this time on the part of Mrs Grace Cooke herself, which is recounted in the original book of THE LIVING WORD. We will tell this story in some detail because it has a strong bearing upon the substance of the book.

Some ten years before the first of the talks in this book was given, at the request of the Polaire Brotherhood (of which the reader can find an account in THE RETURN OF ARTHUR CONAN DOYLE and also in HEALING BY THE SPIRIT, both published by the White Eagle Publishing Trust), she journeyed with a group of the Polaires to the Pyrenees to try to help them by her psychic gifts to find and uncover the hidden treasure of the Albigenses or Cathars. They had been told, through their own magical means of communication with the Sages who had brought their order into being, that this lay buried beneath the castle of Lordat, which lies some twelve kilometres as the crow flies from Montségur, the 'last stronghold' of that persecuted and massacred brotherhood of *bons hommes*. They were furthermore told to seek the help of Mrs Grace Cooke in finding the treasure, and that it would be found within three days of the start of the search. Since the ultimate massacre of the Cathars rumour of an immense treasure hidden in the neighbourhood of Montségur has persisted, for which many an expedition has sought in vain (regardless of the fact that a brotherhood which had abjured all worldly wealth might not desire to accumulate riches). Possibly the Polaires were seeking a greater treasure, in manuscript, which would reveal the lost secret of the Albigenses, the inner substance of their faith.

We will take up the story in Mrs Cooke's own words as they appeared in the first edition of this book in 1949. 'During our stay we climbed each morning to the summit of the mountain [Lordat was a little village high up the mountainside, and the castle stood above it] in the hope of being led to the right spot for beginning excavations.... From the beginning we were strongly impressed by the dual nature of the unseen powers around us. There were times when the dark forces were predominant. Then ... [there] came, like a breath of heaven, a sweet pure, gentle, loving influence like a spiritual illumination, which made us certain of the presence of immortal brothers waiting and watching. At such times as these we felt we were under the protection of great white wings, guarded by a power which must be experienced to be believed. Although we were ... amidst dangerous elemental forces and in the company of unbalanced human minds [one of those making up the Polaire party had become deranged, and had attacked another], we were constantly reminded, by the whispers of the unseen ... that Christ is all-love and his spirit has power to comfort and protect from all harm. This strengthened our will to proceed. Many times this wave of spiritual light and power caused the dark veil between matter and the inner world to become thin, to such a degree that we found ourselves in company with the gentle spirits of the Albigenses, who for centuries had walked this very plateau on which we stood ...

'On the third day after our arrival, when we were idly contemplating the grand panorama of mountains under the intensely blue sky with, in the distance [the path winding away towards], the ancient castle of Montségur, my attention was caught by the sudden appearance of a shining form ... 'Shining' is the only word to describe the aura of the spirit who appeared, but his manner was as normal as that of any human being might be who, while out walking, had stumbled by chance upon a stranger. He appeared simple, kindly, and treated the situation as naturally as if it were customary for discarnate people to talk to men and women. He looked like an old man at first sight; that is to say, he wore a longish white beard and his hair was silver, but, apart from this his skin was youthful and clear, as though a light shone behind the flesh, and his warm blue eyes were alight with an inner fire. He was clothed in white, in the garb of some early order of Christian Brothers and bore himself with noble meekness. "Could this be one of the Albigenses?" I asked mentally. Yes. It was true; by sign and symbol he proved to me that he belonged to this age–old Brotherhood. Why had he appeared in this manner?'

He indicated that he had come to help in the search. However, he said that no material treasure would be found until men were ready to use it, until they had found the spiritual treasure, which was the secret of how their own lower nature could be transformed – the base metal turned into living gold. He indicated that in the life and teachings of Jesus the Christ would be found the key to this spiritual treasure. He spoke of John, the disciple beloved of the Master; how he had not died 'as most men die' but had passed onwards to a higher life in a body of light as his Master had done before him. He had remained on earth for a very long time, travelling to the East and to the West, coming indeed to this very place where he had meditated and communed with his Master. He spoke of the inner mystical teaching from the Master which he, John, had passed on to his followers and which had been handed down through secret brotherhoods through the centuries; and that this mystical gospel

x

was in fact the source and secret of the treasure of the Albigenses. (In this connection it is interesting to note that there is some historical evidence linking the Cathars with early Christian groups.*)

After the visitor had withdrawn into the inner world from which he had come Mrs Cooke 'seemed to live in a haze of happiness for days'. Even today, forty-six years later, she says that the experience remains one of the most vivid and memorable of her life. 'Words could not describe', she says, 'the sweet and wonderful love of this simple Brother.'

As for the Polaires' treasure none was ever discovered. The expedition was ill-equipped for such a venture. At last the task was abandoned, and to all appearances the attempt had been useless and the message of the Sages falsified.

But had it? It was as if the contact with that pure and great brother who had come, she felt, from what she called 'the sphere of St John', had brought about a permanent change of consciousness in the medium, so that thereafter her life's work began to take form. Teaching began to come through her from the world of spirit, through her guide White Eagle, that gradually formed the philosophy of love that has helped and healed souls all over the world, and, in White Eagle's words, 'helped the light in the heart grow' in thousands of lives. The teaching has become a simple revelation of mystical Christianity, which at the same time, transcending the limits of dogma, seemed quietly to bring the wisdom of the East and West together.

The talks embodied in this book came, as we have already said, some ten years after that never wholly forgotten meeting in the foothills of the Pyrenees. We have already described the atmosphere in which the talks were given. Grace Cooke herself has always felt them to be the real fruits of her meeting with that great and pure soul from the 'sphere of St John'. Perhaps I can add, for what it may be worth, in confirmation, that I myself have the clearest memory of a vision which persisted at

---

* See the article by G.M.H. in *Stella Polaris* (magazine of the White Eagle Lodge), vol. v, reprinted in vol. xxvii.

those lectures, and often in my meditations at that time, of a saintly bearded man beside a cave high up in the mountains, who only now as I have had to study the story as originally told, do I recognise to be as I most truly believe, the same saintly one of the meeting at Lordat.

All these events lie behind the actual teachings on the gospel of St John that make up this book, but the teaching stands fully by itself without the story. May it be true nevertheless that those who read White Eagle's words with heart as well as mind may come to find within their own being that treasure beyond all worldly value, of which the gentle brother spoke, which can bring eternal life and happiness to every child of God.

Y.G.H.
March 1979

The First Chapter

SOUL AND SPIRIT

WE BRING a message which we pray will be clear [White Eagle says], for we desire above all to be clear and simple. We will also try to make plain the foundation upon which the teaching of the White Eagle is built. Sometimes there may appear to be paradoxes, even contradictions, for there are many paradoxes on the spiritual path. But be patient; do not jump to conclusions. In time you will find an adequate explanation for every paradox. We would remind you, brethren, of the ancient truths embodied in the bible; that when the bible is read with understanding, when the light of the spirit is thrown upon its pages, you will discover many jewels of truth and indeed, all that man needs for his life here and hereafter.

We are told in the book of Genesis that in six days God created the seas, the earth, and all creatures on earth and in the seas and in the worlds above the earth; and lastly, that He created man in His own image and breathed into man the breath of life (Gen. 1, 2). Thus man became a living soul.

Confusion still exists concerning the nature and functions of the soul and also of the spirit of man. Once spirit comes down to dwell in the flesh it starts to create what is called a soul, for soul is that part of man's being which is built up through experiences undergone by the tender inner self of man during incarnation. Soul can further be described as the feminine aspect of man's life, the mother principle. The soul of the world is made up of the feeling of the world, the soul of a nation is created by the feeling of the people of that nation.

In esoteric teaching you will always find the soul referred to as representing the mother or feminine aspect of life, the second principle – the first principle being divine will, the father or masculine aspect. In Genesis the story is told how the woman is

I

taken from the region of the heart of the first man, Adam; while Adam lay quiescent God brought forth from his 'rib', or heart, the woman – the second principle.

We should learn to recognise the importance of this soul, this woman aspect; lacking a soul, the first principle in man could not continue to evolve. Adam needed that second aspect to complete him. He had to become ensouled to enable him to live fully. Soul gives feeling to the self of man and it is the intuitive part of man. (The coming Age of Aquarius will bring the mother or woman aspect of life into greater prominence. In other words it will usher in greater development of intuition and an increase of soul power among the peoples of the earth.)

The first principle, being representative of the Father or the will, must be balanced by the Mother principle or the intuition. When there is a perfect balance and blending of these two principles, then the Christ-child is brought forth as a perfect outcome of this union.

Do not mistake our meaning; every human being contains both manly and womanly qualities; in one incarnation the male may predominate; in another, the female. Each individual soul passes through many trials, tribulations and initiations, through the process of which these two principles of will and love are becoming united and perfectly harmonised in man and he becomes Christed. This is the true meaning of the immaculate conception, which is the outcome of the mystical marriage between spirit and soul within man.

We are trying to convey (and a very difficult task it is) the nature of the divine Trinity of Father Mother and Son. And we are trying to show the need for that union between spirit and soul in man, and the truth which underlies the teaching of the immaculate conception.

Now we are told that God created man a living soul, but this soul is not necessarily immortal, it is not the eternal part of man. Shall we describe the soul's body as a finer replica of man's physical form?

This soul-body has two aspects – first, that portion which is the bridge between earth and heaven during mortal life but is not itself immortal, for it gradually disintegrates after the death of the body; and second, the part of the soul-body which lives on after physical death, the clothing of the spirit. But not until something happens – and that something is an awakening of the life of the soul by the breath of God – does the soul become truly quickened and live eternally. *And the Lord God formed man of the dust of the ground, and breathed into his nostrils the breath of life; and man became a living soul* (Gen. 2 : 7). This is a spiritual truth not understood by many.

There are those who find that in certain conditions they can receive impressions from the other world through their soul or psyche, and they think that this is the be-all and end-all of the spiritual quest. But no; what they are seeing is only one step beyond the physical. It is merely like contacting something apart from themselves – say a chair, a table, a book – but they are not necessarily contacting spirit. The soul world appears to the soul senses to be as natural and as solid as the physical world is to the physical senses; the only difference being that the soul world has an existence apart from dense matter. The soul can live in that world for centuries, but still needs something more before it can enter eternal life. It needs that quickening by the breath of God, that Christing of man. And it is with this quickening that the gospel of St John deals.

Jesus himself stressed this truth in many of his teachings. If you study the gospel you will find repeated references to it, such as *I am the way, the truth and the life . . . I am the light of the world . . . No man cometh unto the Father, but by me* (Jn. 14 : 6, 8 : 12). This was not Jesus the man speaking but the Christ in him. The Master Jesus provided a channel for the divine and eternal truth of Christ, the way. The more you analyse the sayings of Jesus, the more will this truth of the Christ in him, the eternal life, reveal itself.

The Christ is the eternal life in you too. This is why, in your meditations, you should not allow yourself to linger on the astral or the psychic planes (where doubtless you will see many interesting things) but should aspire to Christ through His light in your heart, which is the light of the world, the eternal, living flame of love.

(1 : 1–5) *In the beginning was the Word, and the Word was with God, and the Word was God. The same was in the beginning with God. All things were made by him; and without him was not any thing made that was made. In him was life; and the life was the light of men. And the light shineth in darkness; and the darkness comprehended it not.*

We would suggest first that the teachings of the four gospels should not be confined to the period of time during which Jesus lived on earth. The truth contained in them was brought to the world in the beginning; it is an eternal truth, repeated to mankind through ages of time.

The creative 'word' is the eternal light shining from the heart of the Father Mother God. It is the Christ the Son. This was the light which shone through Jesus and spoke through him. God is that light; God is the light which shines in the darkness of the earth – we do not mean merely the sun which shines upon the physical earth, but the light which is in all that comprises the life of man on earth. The Word of God, the holy mystical Word, which was love, created form out of chaos and created man, and in man was placed the seed of the Christ man. *In him was life; and the life was the light of men* (4), which means that the light was born in man; it has been in man from the beginning.

(1 : 6–11) *There was a man sent from God whose name was John. The same came for a witness, to bear witness of the Light, that all men through him might believe. He was not that Light, but was sent to bear witness of that Light. That was the true Light which lighteth every man that cometh into the world. He was in the world, and the world was made by him, and the world knew him not. He came unto his own, and his own received him not.*

The purpose of life on this earth planet is that spirit, your spirit, shall shine within the darkness. Your spirit, which is the light which was in the beginning: this means that in the beginning of your existence you were light; and the light shone in the darkness – which is your dense body or the earth – and the earth comprehended it not. You are all familiar with this teaching, but you do not think of it as applying to yourself. You do not understand that in essence you are light; and that in the beginning you were light until you entered the physical body, or that that physical body, and particularly the mortal mind, does not comprehend the light. You are here to use physical matter and not allow it to dominate you. You are light; and you have to shine out through the darkness, to transmute the heavy atoms of the physical body by the light within you. Miracles happen when the spirit has gained such power of control over the body. The spirit becomes so strong in its manipulation of the physical atoms that it can use any of the elements at will.

This is done not only by the mind of earth but by the mind of God. It is done by that pure spiritual consciousness which is all love, which is the spirit.

(1 : 12–13) *But as many as received him, to them gave he power to become the sons of God, even to them that believe on his name: Which were born, not of blood, nor of the will of the flesh, nor of the will of man, but of God.*

Later in the gospel you will read the story of the changing of the water into wine. These verses refer to the same mystery, in symbolic terms. Water represents the psyche or soul before the quickening power of the spirit changes the soul into wine – into light. The whole being of man is quickened, transformed, given eternal life, by spirit, by light; this story implies the breathing into man of the life of the spirit. A soul may undergo many, many incarnations before it becomes thus quickened. But if, as can happen (but rarely) the soul fails to respond to the quickening light and instead sinks lower and lower, it becomes ever more responsive to negative forces, or what is called evil, and is eventually self-destroyed. The soul is destroyed; but the spirit is eternal and will be breathed forth again to make again its soul clothing. There is within us all an urge towards divinity, towards truth and love; this is the source of all aspiration. The soul can respond to this urge or can ignore it; while it is neglected, the soul will remain in darkness. But with the soul's response will come a quickening of the divine life within, which bestows eternal life upon the soul. The eternal soul is born, *not of blood, nor of the will of the flesh, nor of the will of man, but of God* (of the divine spirit).

(1 : 14) *And the Word was made flesh, and dwelt among us (and we beheld his glory, the glory as of the only begotten of the Father,) full of grace and truth.*

The Word was God! The Word dwelt in the flesh, in man. It dwelt in the flesh of Jesus, who was to be teacher and revealer of eternal truth to man.

(1 : 15–34) *John bare witness of him, and cried, saying, This was he of whom I spake, He that cometh after me is preferred before me: for he was before me. And of his fulness have all we received, and grace for grace. For the law was given by Moses, but grace and truth came by Jesus Christ. No man hath seen God at any time; the only begotten Son, which is in the bosom of the Father, he hath declared him.*

And this is the record of John, when the Jews sent priests and Levites from Jerusalem to ask him, Who art Thou? And he confessed and denied not; but confessed, I am not the Christ. And they asked him, What then? Art thou Elias? And he saith, I am not. Art thou that prophet? And he answered, No. Then said they unto him, Who art thou? that we may give an answer to them that sent us. What sayest thou of thyself?

He said, I am the voice of one crying in the wilderness, Make straight the way of the Lord, as said the prophet Esaias.

And they which were sent were of the Pharisees. And they asked him, and said unto him, Why baptizest thou then, if thou be not that Christ, nor Elias, neither that prophet?

John answered them, saying, I baptize with water; but there

standeth one among you, whom ye know not; He it is, who coming
after me is preferred before me, whose shoe's latchet I am not worthy
to unloose.

These things were done in Bethabara beyond Jordan, where John
was baptizing. The next day John seeth Jesus coming unto him, and
saith, Behold the Lamb of God, which taketh away the sin of the
world. This is he of whom I said, After me cometh a man which is
preferred before me: for he was before me. And I knew him not: but
that he should be made manifest to Israel, therefore am I come
baptizing with water. And John bare record, saying, I saw the
Spirit descending from heaven like a dove, and it abode upon him.
And I knew him not: but he that sent me to baptize with water, the
same said unto me, Upon whom thou shalt see the Spirit descending,
and remaining on him, the same is he which baptizeth with the Holy
Ghost. And I saw, and bare record that this is the Son of God.

Notice that emphasis is laid upon the statement of John the
Baptist that Jesus was older far than he, John. *He was before me*
(30), said John. In this statement we read the meaning that Jesus
was older in soul than the earth itself; we perceive that Jesus
lived before the creation of the earth, that is to say before the
human family peopled the earth. And he was a channel, pure
and holy, through which the Christ the perfect and only begotten Son of the Father Mother God, was born – and continues
to be born throughout the ages of mankind. It is evident that
John recognised the presence of Christ the Son of God in Jesus.

He it is, who coming after me is preferred before me, whose shoe's
latchet I am not worthy to unloose (27). John came into the wilderness – the mass of confused thought, the wilderness of ignorance – to make ready for the coming of the Lord. John comes
to prepare men's minds and souls for the coming of the Christ:
I baptise with water, he said, but he will baptise with spirit.*

This is interesting. We have already likened the element water
to the soul. Now water is also to be regarded as a purifier of the
soul. The soul of man, as we have already said, is not the same

* See appendix, p. 186, 'Baptism'.

7

as the spirit; it is the clothing of the spirit, the bridge between the physical body and the divine spirit. Because it is the clothing of the spirit, it contains an element of the divine, there is that in it which enables it to respond to pure and beautiful vibrations and thus to penetrate into higher spheres. Coarser elements are also built into the structure of the soul as the result of man's response to lower and more animal instincts. This lower part of the soul is closely interwoven with the physical body and will disintegrate at the end of each incarnation, while the higher part remains and is absorbed into that soul-body or 'temple' which has been in construction since the beginning of time.

Man's soul is comprised of the astral, the mental and the celestial body; that is all the soul. But there is something else; there is the spirit. Now, when the soul has garnered all the experience it can from the physical life so that it is ready to pass on into the Christ initiation, there is a wonderful 'resurrection', or enlightenment, or awakening waiting for it. The Christ in man becomes conscious, stirs, awakens. Jesus was the great initiate for the manifestation of this Christ spirit. Jesus became the Christed one. He trod the path and demonstrated to humanity the way. He said: 'I am that way, that truth and life'. Jesus demonstrated to the rest of humanity the way to life eternal. Jesus Christ was not the only Christed one but he did demonstrate the way of purification of all the vehicles including the physical, for every soul.

John refers to John the Baptist, he who baptises with the water which purifies and cleanses the psyche, the soul, with its accumulation of karma. But was there not one coming, who would baptise with the spirit, the divine spirit . . . the Christ, the light, the word, which shines in the darkness of you all, in us all? He baptises with that tremendous fire, the fire of divine life, the very life within the soul; and unless the soul responds, the soul is dead, is in the darkness.

Christ is the great initiator into the mysteries of the divine fire in man. The divine fire in man is pure love, the Christ love, that which is born – not that which was born, that which is born

8

– of the Father Mother God; the only-begotten Son is the divine spirit or fire, the perfect love.

(1 : 35–6) *Again the next day after John stood, and two of his disciples; And looking upon Jesus as he walked, he saith, Behold the Lamb of God!*

Behold the Lamb of God! What was meant exactly by this phrase? To the Jews the lamb was associated with sacrifice in the temple. At first this sounds somewhat crude, but we go deeper and realise that what is meant here by sacrifice is a subjection of the instincts of the lower self. There is no one except Jesus who has sacrificed his entire self to God; but John could see – being a prophet and a seer – that Jesus was such a man. Having surrendered his whole nature, he had no self-will, no desires. He had sacrificed or relinquished everything within that temple which was his human form, to the incoming Christ, to God. John called him 'the Lamb of God' because he had surrendered everything of this lower nature to the divine spirit, to God. *The Lamb of God, which taketh away the sin of the world* (29) – the pure and perfect soul or psyche of Jesus Christ, perfect in its purity and simplicity, free from karma, which had been prepared through ages of time for this divine revelation to humanity that every man had within him the power, the light; and if man responded to that light which rested on the face of the water, the still water of his own soul deep within his own being, he would enter into the kingdom of God, the kingdom of eternity.

He had laid down his life, but he that giveth his life (who gives himself utterly) shall receive eternal life. Do you see what this means? When the life of the soul or psyche, which is temporal, is laid aside so that that divine and eternal life of Christ can enter, that soul is saved or quickened to eternal life. You may say here, 'But we know that life continues after death, that the soul goes on and on, that man cannot die, cannot be destroyed'. But can you not see a deeper truth – that life becomes eternal only when the divine spirit or divine fire purifies and redeems the psyche, quickens its vibrations, transmutes its elements, and raises it to heaven?

(1 : 38–9) *Then Jesus turned, and saw them following, and saith unto them, What seek ye? They said unto him, Rabbi (which is to say, being interpreted, Master), where dwellest thou? He saith unto them, Come and see. They came and saw where he dwelt, and abode with him that day: for it was about the tenth hour.*

When the disciples asked Jesus where he lived, he answered, *Come and see.* Yet elsewhere we are told that Jesus had nowhere to lay his head. We read into this paradox this meaning – that Jesus lived constantly with his Father in heaven (which was his true abode), in a condition which you may endeavour in meditation to touch, if only for a flash, when some inner stimulus draws you up to a place beyond power of description, but which intuition tells you is your spiritual home. Jesus dwelt there constantly. As you develop, through meditation; as you reach to that place of holiness, great light and beauty, gradually you will be able to increase the duration of your stay. In the beginning you will only vaguely be conscious of it, then in a flash, you will touch the true glory; as time goes on you will be able to remain longer. There are still great teachers, called avatars, who can enter into this state of bliss. So great was Jesus that he was able to remain indefinitely in this state of heavenly consciousness. You will notice that the disciples went with Jesus and dwelt with him awhile; in other words, by the light and glory emanating from him he was able so to quicken the disciples' consciousness that they too could dwell with him for a while in the heavenly state. Through his power and love he was able to impart this gift of vision. The spiritual teacher of today, in lesser degree, can also enable his disciple to raise his consciousness, which is why a teacher can prove so helpful. Of course, as Jesus said again and again – *the Father that dwelleth in me, he doeth the works. I do nothing of myself* (Jn. 14 : 10, 8 : 28). He was merely the channel, pure and perfected, for the manifestation of the God in man which touches and raises the disciple to the vision glorious.

10

(1 : 40–2) *One of the two which heard John speak, and followed him, was Andrew, Simon Peter's brother. He first findeth his own brother Simon, and saith unto him, We have found the Messias, which is, being interpreted, the Christ. And he brought him to Jesus. And when Jesus beheld him, he said, Thou art Simon the son of Jona: thou shalt be called Cephas, which is by interpretation, a stone.*

That naming of Simon as a stone is interesting and suggests that Simon at that time was a man of strong mentality, strong intellect. Although Jesus knew that there was great good in Simon, he called him a stone because he was so unresponsive. There is life indwelling in the stone, but it is difficult to get at it! This recalls another saying of the Master, when he referred to the very stones crying out (Lk. 19 : 40). Here we have it again, you see – a power so great that it must win a response even from those as hard as stone.

(1 : 43–51) *The day following Jesus would go forth into Galilee, and findeth Philip, and saith unto him, Follow me. Now Philip was of Bethsaida, the city of Andrew and Peter. Philip findeth Nathanael, and saith unto him, We have found him, of whom Moses in the law, and the prophets, did write, Jesus of Nazareth, the son of Joseph. And Nathanael said unto him, Can there any good thing come out of Nazareth? Philip saith unto him, Come and see.*

Jesus saw Nathanael coming to him, and saith of him, Behold an Israelite indeed, in whom is no guile! Nathanael saith unto him, Whence knowest thou me? Jesus answered and said unto him, Before that Philip called thee, when thou wast under the fig tree, I saw thee.

Nathanael answered and saith unto him, Rabbi, thou art the Son of God; thou art the King of Israel.

Jesus answered and said unto him, Because I said unto thee, I saw thee under the fig tree, believest thou? thou shalt see greater things than these. And he saith unto him, Verily, verily, I say unto you, Hereafter ye shall see heaven open, and the angels of God ascending and descending upon the Son of man.

In these few verses we can read yet another truth.

How pleased and excited Nathanael became when Jesus demonstrated the power of his clairvoyant vision by seeing him under the fig tree! Nathanael was overwhelmed by this and thought that surely only a God-like power could see at such a distance. In our spiritual youth, we are likewise impressed with very ordinary psychic happenings. Having witnessed them, we are inclined to think we have nothing else to learn, and there we stop. But psychic powers, of themselves, are not enough; the possession of psychic powers does not make a master or even a wise man. Jesus had perfectly developed psychic powers, but also something more. He had developed true spiritual perception. Not only could he see Nathanael under the fig tree, as in a vision, but he could also read Nathanael's soul, and knew exactly how far he had travelled along the evolutionary path. We mention this because it has been said that Jesus was an ordinary medium, but this statement is only a half truth at the most; Jesus was a perfectly evolved being, a perfected soul who had developed to the fullest degree the hidden powers latent within man. The difference between Jesus and the ordinary psychic is that the psychic elements in Jesus were transmuted into the heavenly.

You must not think that we are decrying psychic gifts. We would only make it clear that they come into the natural course of evolution. They are not the be-all and end-all; they have their place, but they are very ordinary. The soul must reach beyond psychic gifts.

And he saith unto him, Verily, verily, I say unto you, Hereafter ye shall see heaven open, and the angels of God ascending and descending upon the Son of man (51). In these words Jesus goes on to describe what lies beyond psychic development, that beyond psychic development there was something more to be striven for. We interpret this to mean that when man sits devotedly in meditation and contemplation and opens his heart to the inflow of divine love, he will become so raised in consciousness that he will behold the angels of God. He will attain to that state of ecstasy where he will keep company with angels. Here is the true spiritual gift. Here is the true goal, my friends, not merely the development of any sixth sense or psychic power, which is as nothing compared with this baptism, this raising of the spirit, this bringing forth of the divine fire of the spirit from the heart; for then the soul will behold the angel hosts and will dwell in its true home, the abode of Christ.

The Second Chapter

THE WATER AND THE WINE

WE COME to help you to realise more fully the way, the truth and the life of the eternal spirit. There is no new truth; all that is contained in the teaching of the gospels we received long ages ago in the temple of the Great White Light. There we learnt the same story of the psyche (the soul) and of the divine fire, the divine spirit, which comes from God, the Father Mother, to illumine the soul. This ancient wisdom has been given to mankind again and again through many teachers; and in Christianity itself we find another presentation of the eternal truth.

Unfortunately the mind, which is the slayer of the real, takes the word of the Master and misinterprets the meaning. Throughout the gospels we can trace this same misinterpretation of mystical truth and upon this misrepresentation has been built an edifice, the windows of which are opaque, and men are unable fully to understand the message of the Master.

The greatest enemy to man's spiritual progress is his mind. We recognise that mind can also be his friend, because through mind he can receive and understand truth. But mind must always be guided by the divine spirit in the heart, the spirit of Christ, humble, meek, lowly and lovely. Divine love in the heart flashes forth as a light to illumine the mind and give that clear vision which can reveal heaven and hell to man. The purpose of life is for man to manifest the divine fire on earth, through his physical body.

We shall now speak of the second chapter of the gospel, with special reference to the miracle of the changing of the water into wine.

(2 : 1–25) *And the third day there was a marriage in Cana of Galilee; and the mother of Jesus was there: And both Jesus was*

called, and his disciples, to the marriage. And when they wanted wine, the mother of Jesus saith unto him, They have no wine. Jesus saith unto her, Woman, what have I to do with thee? mine hour is not yet come. His mother saith unto the servants, Whatsoever he saith unto you, do it.

And there were set there six waterpots of stone, after the manner of the purifying of the Jews, containing two or three firkins apiece. Jesus saith unto them, Fill the waterpots with water. And they filled them up to the brim. And he saith unto them, Draw out now, and bear unto the governor of the feast. And they bare it. When the ruler of the feast had tasted the water that was made wine, and knew not whence it was: (but the servants which drew the water knew); the governor of the feast called the bridegroom, and saith unto him, Every man at the beginning doth set forth good wine; and when men have well drunk, then that which is worse; but thou hast kept the good wine until now.

This beginning of miracles did Jesus in Cana of Galilee, and manifested forth his glory; and his disciples believed on him. After this he went down to Capernaum, he, and his mother, and his brethren, and his disciples: and they continued there not many days.

And the Jews' passover was at hand, and Jesus went up to Jerusalem, and found in the temple those that sold oxen and sheep and doves, and the changers of money sitting. And when he had made a scourge of small cords, he drove them all out of the temple, and the sheep, and the oxen; and poured out the changers' money, and overthrew the tables; And said unto them that sold doves, Take these things hence; make not my Father's house an house of merchandise. And his disciples remembered that it was written, The zeal of thine house hath eaten me up.

Then answered the Jews and said unto him, What sign shewest thou unto us, seeing that thou doest these things? Jesus answered and said unto them, Destroy this temple, and in three days I will raise it up. Then said the Jews, Forty and six years was this temple in building, and wilt thou rear it up in three days? But he spake of the temple of his body. When therefore he was risen from the dead, his

*disciples remembered that he had said this unto them; and they
believed the scriptures, and the word which Jesus had said.*

*Now when he was in Jerusalem at the passover, in the feast day,
many believed in his name, when they saw the miracles which he did.
But Jesus did not commit himself unto them, because he knew all
men, and needed not that any should testify of man: for he knew
what was in man.*

Now water is an ancient symbol frequently employed by Jesus
to impart mystical truth to his brethren. In the science of astrol-
ogy the signs of the zodiac coming under the water element
are said to be linked with the psyche, and in mystical teaching
water is always symbolic of the soul. The psyche at its source is
like pure water; but as it descends and becomes clothed with the
physical body it may become, as it were, muddy, opaque, heavy;
yet it flows on and eventually runs clean again when it rejoins
the great ocean of divine consciousness, the universal psyche or
soul. The psyche of the individual man may be pure and clean,
or it may be murky and discoloured, according to his stage of
spiritual evolution. The water symbol always represents the
soul.

At the wedding feast at Cana his mother called to Jesus,
saying, *They have no wine* (3), and Jesus answered, apparently
rather sharply, *Woman, what have I to do with thee?* (4). We
suggest that these words are a mistranslation. What we think was
meant was, 'Woman (my companion, my sister), let us share
what we have; what is mine is thine too, therefore we share it.
Bring me the jars containing the water, we will share what we
have'. What they had in common was the spirit of Christ. And
so, from the universal or cosmic consciousness this divine fire,
this divine essence, the wine of life itself passed through the
Master to the souls of others present. Through the Christ spirit,
the water (or the soul) is changed into the wine, it is infused
with the divine fire of eternal life, the Christ life. This is what
the mediaeval mystics called the mystical marriage. Do you remember, when Jesus hung on the cross, his side was pierced by

16

the soldier's spear, and water and blood flowed from the wound? This is another symbol of the mystical marriage, the marriage of the psyche or the soul, and the divine spirit, the Son.

You will remember that at the marriage feast one of the guests said to the bridegroom: 'Why! You have saved your best wine (wine which apparently had been created by a miracle) to the end!' There is mystical meaning here also. For at the end of man's life on earth, when the soul leaves the body, a change takes place in the elements of that psyche; and the Christ spirit, entering into the psyche in its changed state, brings about a more exquisite blending, or produces more exquisite 'wine' than is possible while the psyche is enchained in the physical body. And so it is at the end of mortal life that the most beautiful wine is brought forth for mankind.

On another occasion Jesus said: *Neither do men put new wine into old bottles* (Mt. 9 : 17). What was meant by that? The old bottle – the earth-tired psyche – has to be transmuted and puri- fied before it can receive this new and perfect wine of divine consciousness. Is not this a comforting, a glorious message? It is suggested that man cannot progress towards realisation of cosmic consciousness until he lives to serve and share with all men whatever blessing comes to him. This again is mystical truth, this sharing the wine of the universal life, that divine blessing which flows into the heart. We suggest that the awaken- ing of the Christ light makes the bridge between the individual consciousness and the universal. The soul is the individual con- sciousness. The Christ spirit in the heart, as it develops and grows, unites the individual with the universal or with the cosmos. The Christ spirit is the bridge between the individual and the universal consciousness.

This is how prayers are answered. God is all love and all wisdom; it is impossible to describe His glory, and each indivi- dual must himself seek and find this love. But when the soul prays to its Father Mother, asking not for anything of a selfish nature, but only for that which it can share with others, it is bound to receive an answer, because the pure and true love from the Father Mother enters the heart of the child. Because the child prays for good, prays to be about his Father's business, with the will to share with his fellows all that comes, he makes himself or herself a channel for divine love, and as divine love flows into his heart there comes the answer to his prayer.

Remember, these truths must find expression on every plane of consciousness, even to the outermost ring of the physical and the material life. Life is one whole and all its parts are most harmoniously blended, and this divine fire must manifest on each plane right down to the physical. This is why there appear to be so many interpretations of truth. There is only one truth really, but it finds manifestation, at many different levels. But we are concerned with the original source of this river of truth – God.

Do you recall the reference in the Revelation of St John to *a pure river of water of life . . . proceeding out of the throne of God* (Rev. 22 : 1)? The river of the water of life is the great universal psyche outflowing from God, and finding manifestation in many different forms. Jesus said: *In my Father's house are many mansions* (Jn. 14 : 2). This is sometimes interpreted to mean the many different homes in the spirit world. We do not deny this interpretation, but we also suggest that there are many mansions in man's being, many vehicles through which God manifests – the physical, the mental, the emotional, the intuitional and the rest. These are the many mansions, this is 'my Father's house' – the whole of man's being. In ancient days we called it the 'temple'.

The 'many mansions' calls to mind another saying of Jesus when he told Peter: *That thou art Peter; and upon this rock I will build my church . . . and whatsoever thou shalt loose on earth shall be loosed in heaven* (Mt.16 : 18–19). There has been much speculation as to the real meaning of these words. The church referred to here is not a body of men. It is misleading in this context to think of a church as a group of people who congregate to worship God. 'Thou art Peter – the man, Peter – and upon thee will I build my church.' 'My church' is the cosmic, universal temple of worship, and the temple of worship in the heart of every man. *Whatsoever thou shalt bind* to thyself *on earth*, in the earth-life, *shall be bound in heaven* (Mt. 16 : 19). Jesus hid deep mystical meaning in these words. The church in Peter was the true worship of God in his heart. Upon the truth that was in the man, Peter, would he build his church. And whatsoever a man binds to himself on earth shall be bound to him in heaven; and whatsoever he shall loose, or release, or conquer in himself on earth, he shall find released in himself in heaven.

Jesus walked upon the water – he stilled the storm on the sea. This indicates that the Christ in Jesus had control over his emotional body, over his soul body, the psyche. Christ in him could not be drawn down into the confusion of the psyche, he rose above confused emotions, he stilled the water. When the storm rose, he commanded the air and the water spirits to be still; he stilled the storm of the psyche, or of the souls of his disciples, he stilled the storm of emotion. Christ is Master and controls all heaven and earth, and makes the soul still.

The greatest thing in life is love. Not a lip service to love; he that doeth the will of my Father in heaven, not he who crieth Lord, Lord. The service of love, the sharing of all with all, the pouring forth from the heart of true Christ love; the recognition of the dignity of every living soul, the dignity of the animal world; being at all times ready and able to see, to hear, to taste, to smell and touch the divine life of God – this is the way to Christ, to the cosmic consciousness. Christ is the saviour of mankind – not the man Jesus, but the universal Christ of all ages. Universal love is the saviour of mankind. This is our message.

The Third Chapter

THE COMING OF THE SAVIOUR

EVER SINCE Jesus spoke of the coming of the Comforter, men have yearned for that Comforter. Millions of aspiring Christians are still looking, still waiting; but their spiritual eyes are closed, and they do not yet understand what was meant.

In the course of our talks together we hope to make the meaning clear; for when we look across the world and see the sorrow and suffering of mankind, we know how great is man's need for comfort. You, in common with all humanity, experience loneliness and sickness of mind and body; you suffer because of the absence of something in your life. What is it? The spirit, the fire, the love, the companionship of the spirit. You feel alone, separated, and are filled with unnameable longing.

The Comforter is clearly revealed in the teachings of Jesus, the teachings of that Christ spirit which has shone forth in varying degrees through spiritual leaders and teachers throughout the history of mankind. In the Christian teaching, once it can be understood by the Western world, can be found a clear story of human life, revealing the nature of the soul and spirit of man, and of the laws which govern all life, including the laws of reincarnation and karma; and, crowning all, a revelation of the Comforter, the divine spirit.

When John the Baptist spoke of Jesus baptising not with water but with fire (Mt. 3 : 11), he meant the fire of the holy spirit, that light coming from heaven, by whose agency a man can be born again. Although already born of the elements, in his physical body and in his psychic or soul body, he is not yet born from above, or born of the spirit, until the divine baptism takes place.

As we proceed we shall see two distinct aspects of man referred to again and again in parable, miracle and in teaching by word: on the one hand the soul or psyche, and on the other, the spirit, or divine fire. These two aspects are not yet clear in orthodox teaching; many words are used, leading only to confusion. But from this confusion, let us extricate one vital word, repeated again and again and again, and always seeming to be allied with the Christ spirit – that word is *love*. Even love is not understood, because it has many facets, many interpretations; the earnest and simple Christian, however, tries according to his understanding to obey Jesus' injunction to *love one another*: the true Christian strives to be loving. But how lamentably does he sometimes fail when it comes to any unusual test of brotherhood; when, for instance, it comes to the question of war! Always there is some excuse. He says it is difficult to be brotherly when there is so much involved, so many things to consider. He talks about a 'righteous war' and holds that he is justified in defending himself. 'It may be all very well in the future', he says, 'but man has yet to evolve to the Christian stage. Centuries hence, perhaps, we shall be able to practise brotherhood, and so abolish war'. Did Jesus mean no more than this, my brethren – that love and brotherhood should come in some far distant future, when the soul of man had so evolved that it could then easily obey divine law? We do not think so at all.*

The two aspects of which we have spoken – on the one hand body and soul (the flesh and the water), and on the other the divine spirit, the Son of God, are clearly indicated in this third chapter of St John. Jesus came to reveal to man his true nature. Every soul is a child of God. Jesus did not say that he alone possessed miraculous powers. He did not claim that he was different and far above you, but taught that all are born of God and by the same spirit can all be raised up to God. Not only the Lord Jesus but all men are born in the flesh to be born again from heaven. *The Father that dwelleth in me, he doeth the works . . . He that believeth on me, the works that I do shall he do also; and greater works than these shall he do* (Jn. 14 : 10, 12). These miracles are not wrought by a human mind, nor by a powerful intellect, but by the spirit of Christ manifesting in the life.

* Cf. Appendix, p. 189, 'Warfare'.

21

Those who have received the message of truth must *live* that message. Teaching by word of mouth can become vain, but a life that is manifesting the truth, that is demonstrating the spiritual law, stands out as a living example of truth. In this is the power of the Christ message.

Jesus not only preached, but he demonstrated the power of light. The light shone through him. He radiated the light wherever he went. He was attuned at all times to his Father in heaven, to the Great Spirit; because of this he was strong in the spirit of his Father, and continually called upon his heavenly Father to help him to manifest and to demonstrate the light.

To those of you unfamiliar with our teaching we would explain what is meant by 'light'. Light is love. He who is a man of light is a man of love and goodwill, thinking no evil, thinking only good. He obeys the law of the good, the true and the beautiful. He is thereby living the life of the Christ.

The Christ speaking through Jesus said also: *I am the light of the world* (Jn. 8 : 12). I AM. What did he mean by this? Did he mean that he, the personal Jesus, was the light of the world? This is the interpretation of the orthodox church. But was he not referring to the spark within man known throughout the spiritual world as the 'I AM'? Before the world was I AM. I AM the light of the world. I AM the light of life. I AM the light, the love, within your own breast. I and the Father are one. Man has to learn how to contact that I AM which is within; he has to learn to receive the life-force continually flowing into the soul of man, to know the glory of the Father within himself and to manifest that glory. Then he will be filled with light, health, joy and happiness, and will create for himself and for all men a new heaven and a new earth.

Now let us read this third chapter together, taking notice of every word.

(3 : 1–10) *There was a man of the Pharisees, named Nicodemus, a ruler of the Jews: The same came to Jesus by night, and said unto him, Rabbi, we know that thou art a teacher come from God: for no*

*man can do these miracles that thou doest, except God be with
him.*

*Jesus answered and said unto him, Verily, verily, I say unto thee,
Except a man be born again, he cannot see the kingdom of God.*

*Nicodemus saith unto him, How can a man be born when he is old?
can he enter the second time into his mother's womb, and be born?*

*Jesus answered, Verily, verily, I say unto thee, Except a man be
born of water and of the Spirit, he cannot enter into the kingdom of
God. That which is born of the flesh is flesh; and that which is born
of the Spirit is spirit. Marvel not that I said unto thee, Ye must be
born again. The wind bloweth where it listeth, and thou hearest the
sound thereof, but canst not tell whence it cometh, and whither it
goeth: so is every one that is born of the Spirit.*

*Nicodemus answered and said unto him, How can these things
be?*

*Jesus answered and said unto him, Art thou a master of Israel,
and knowest not these things?*

Except a man be born of water and of the Spirit (5) . . . In
mystical teaching, water is always symbolic of the psyche, or the
soul; the spirit is the divine fire. Up to a certain point, man is of
the soul only, and not of the spirit. That is to say, the spirit is
there with the birth, but the soul remains in a state of darkness
until it becomes quickened by and aware of the spirit. The soul
is the clothing of the spirit, and can be stimulated from within so
that it can rise and unite with the spirit. In course of time, the
soul and spirit will unite and become one. In the earlier stages of
his earthly journey man is evolving on the two outermost planes,
the physical and the psychic, and in so doing he gains experience
and finally is born again, born of spirit, as he turns in earnest to
seek God. Many, many souls are living in darkness at the present
time. The elder brethren are trying by their love and help to
awaken these 'dead' souls and bring them to life.

The wind bloweth where it listeth (8) . . . 'the wind' is yet another
reference to the spirit, the divine breath. Blowing whither it will,
it cannot be confined. No man hath seen the spirit. Man daily

sees a manifestation of the psyche, the soul body, which is continually expressing itself through the physical, but he does not see the spirit. Yet the spirit can be felt. . . . You sit quietly in meditation and become aware of the breath of spirit, indescribable and intangible. The wind, the divine breath, bloweth where it listeth.

You notice that Jesus said to Nicodemus, as if in surprise, *Art thou a master of Israel, and knowest not these things?* (10). There are those, even today, who speak purely from the intellect, having much knowledge, but the sweet essence of spirit expressed through tenderness, love and wisdom, they know not. Jesus was at pains to teach his disciples the difference between the knowledge which was of the earthly mind, and the great truth of the Comforter. When the Comforter comes to man, man is reborn; the heavens become open to him, the power of love flows in and through him, and brings gifts of healing, wisdom, power to comfort, power to illumine and to raise others on the wings of spirit.

You will perhaps remember our references to Nathanael and the fig tree, and how stress was laid upon the vision by which Jesus saw Nathanael. The disciples thought it wonderful; but Jesus said, in effect, 'It is nothing – only a psychic vision. Wait until you can see angels ascending and descending from heaven'. This is an experience which can come during times of deep meditation, when the soul is highly attuned and reflects the true vision of heaven. True visions of the spirit do not come through development of psychic power. Psychic power enables people to see disembodied spirits, to see into an astral world closely connected with the physical; but the heavens are not to be reached by psychic power, or revealed by psychic vision. This is the difference to which Jesus referred in regard to his vision of Nathanael.

The same with Nicodemus: Nicodemus was a man of knowledge, possessing a powerful intellect, but he lacked spiritual vision and was thus limited. Some think that when Jesus said man *must be born again* (7) it may perhaps bear a reference to reincarnation; we do not put this interpretation on the words. We understand them to mean that man can, when he is ready, find a new birth.

(3 : 11–15) *Verily, verily, I say unto thee, We speak that we do know, and testify that we have seen; and ye receive not our witness. If I have told you earthly things, and ye believe not, how shall ye believe, if I tell you of heavenly things? And no man hath ascended up to heaven, but he that came down from heaven, even the Son of man which is in heaven. And as Moses lifted up the serpent in the wilderness, even so must the Son of man be lifted up: That whosoever believeth in him should not perish, but have eternal life.*

We draw your attention to the saying, *As Moses lifted up the serpent in the wilderness, even so must the Son of man be lifted up* (14). The Son of man means man that is born of the flesh. The souls of men must be lifted up by a new birth . . . a new birth, when the divine fire is raised in them. As Christ, through Jesus, said, *I, if I be lifted up from the earth, will draw all men unto me* (Jn. 12:32). I, Christ, the Son of God, Christ the indweller, was in Jesus; thus Jesus was both the Son of God and the Son of man, both divine and human.

We have often told you the purpose of man's incarnation, of man's life here on the earth. Through pain, perhaps, and also through joy and happiness man has slowly to develop his higher body, referred to by many of the saints and masters of past and present; the body of light known as the solar body, or the celestial body, as the Master Paul called it. Growth and development and full birth of this divine self or God-self in man is a slow process, but it is the purpose of your life.

As Moses lifted up the serpent in the wilderness (14) . . . The serpent is symbolic of the sacred fire of kundalini, the solar force which, curled as a snake at the base of the spine, lies dormant in most people, waiting to be awakened. This solar force, this creative power has to be raised up into the head and the heart, under the full control of the spirit; or through the Word (the Word of God, which is love), so that man becomes not a man of earth but of eternal life. This is the coming of the supreme Son, the light, the life, in the form of Christ through Jesus. Although this light had been demonstrated through other initiates in the past, there came through Jesus this full manifestation of the Christ life. The solar body of Jesus had been brought to perfection; the Christ light manifested through him and spoke with authority, saying *I am the way, the truth and the life* (Jn. 14 : 6). That was this solar force, this divine life in him, which was speaking. Thus the raising by Moses of the serpent in the wilderness was symbolic of the raising up of Christ in the world; and also symbolic of the raising of the power of kundalini, the 'serpent' power, or the transmutation of the creative force of the body from the lower centres to the heart and the head.

In the age of Aquarius into which we are now advancing, there will come to the earth a great baptism of the spiritual Sun, there will come a great stimulation of the holy, the divine fire, the Christ spirit in the heart of all peoples. You may say it is a long way ahead. You cannot be sure. We cannot; we do not know, but we do know the spiritual laws which govern life. We know that the law is for the serpent fire gradually to rise and illumine man's mind and his heart. We know that man's heart will then be filled with kindliness, with love for God and his fellow creatures.

(3 : 15–16) *That whosoever believeth in him should not perish, but have eternal life. For God so loved the world that he gave his only begotten Son, that whosoever believeth in him should not perish, but have everlasting life.*

'I am the life, I, Christ, the Son of God – I am the life.' So when that life is born into man, he inherits eternal life, because it *is* eternal life. The soul of itself is not eternal, but the divine spirit, the Son of God quickening within, can bestow eternal life upon it. Only when this birth from above takes place does the soul become eternal.

Again Jesus gave the teaching concerning eternal life: 'Except ye believe in me . . . Believe me that I am in the Father and the

26

Father in me ... Believe on me and ye shall be saved. I come to give you life; I come to bring you out of darkness into light; *I am the resurrection, and the life'* (Jn. 11 : 25). Do you not see, my children, in the death of the physical body the great promise of the coming of the solar being, the solar body? The physical, earthly body, the lower aspect of man, dies; but that supreme solar body which is being brought into being, which is developing and evolving through incarnation after incarnation is leading man eventually to eternal life. Man does not enter upon eternal life until the full consciousness of the Christ life is born in him, until he has developed his solar body. This is the way that all men must tread. The Christ speaking through Jesus made it so plain: 'I come that ye might have eternal life' – the solar force, the Christ life and light. I come into you that you may use this creative force, become a being of light. I come that you may become master of your life, of your body, of your conditions, of your circumstances in the world. *I am the way, the truth and the life* (Jn. 14:6).

(3 : 17–28) *For God sent not his Son into the world to condemn the world; but that the world through him might be saved. He that believeth on him is not condemned: but he that believeth not is condemned already, because he hath not believed in the name of the only begotten Son of God. And this is the condemnation, that light is come into the world, and men loved darkness rather than light, because their deeds were evil. For every one that doeth evil hateth the light, neither cometh to the light, lest his deeds should be reproved. But he that doeth truth cometh to the light, that his deeds may be made manifest, that they are wrought in God.*

After these things came Jesus and his disciples into the land of Judaea; and there he tarried with them and baptized. And John also was baptizing in Aenon near to Salim, because there was much water there: and they came, and were baptized. For John was not yet cast into prison. Then there arose a question between some of John's disciples and the Jews about purifying. And they came unto John, and said unto him, Rabbi, he that was with thee beyond

Jordan, to whom thou barest witness, behold, the same baptizeth, and all men come to him.

John answered and said, A man can receive nothing, except it be given him from heaven. Ye yourselves bear me witness, that I said, I am not the Christ, but that I am sent before him.

Orthodoxy conveys the idea that Jesus the man was saviour of mankind, instead of proclaiming to the world that the divine limitless Spirit is the true Son of God and saviour of men, the divine fire born into souls to quicken them, throughout all time. 'As it was in the beginning, is now and ever shall be . . .' Do not limit this birth of the Christ spirit to an event of two thousand years ago. Jesus the great master came to testify this truth and live it himself. He was not himself the Saviour. The Christ in Jesus bore testimony. The Christ who spoke through Jesus was the Son of God, but the Son of God is also universal, the quickening fire born in the collective heart of humanity, and in this sense Christ is the redeemer, the saviour. Those who believe that every man must be his own saviour are both right and wrong – wrong in so far as they lack the inner knowledge to know the difference between the soul and the spirit; wrong also because they think that by themselves they can accomplish so great a thing. But they are right in the sense that every man must become host to the Son of God, must be born again of the spirit.

(3 : 29–36. John the Baptist continues:) *He that hath the bride is the bridegroom: but the friend of the bridegroom, which standeth and heareth him, rejoiceth greatly because of the bridegroom's voice: this my joy therefore is fulfilled. He must increase, but I must decrease. He that cometh from above is above all: he that is of the earth is earthly, and speaketh of the earth: he that cometh from heaven is above all. And what he hath seen and heard, that he testifieth; and no man receiveth his testimony. He that hath received his testimony hath set to his seal that God is true. For he whom God hath sent speaketh the words of God: for God giveth not the Spirit by measure unto him. The Father loveth the Son, and hath given all*

things into his hand. He that believeth on the Son hath everlasting life: and he that believeth not the Son shall not see life; but the wrath of God abideth on him.

The bridegroom is really another term for the Christ spirit. Here again is a reference to the mystic marriage between spirit and soul, between the bridegroom and the bride. How can the bride (the soul) wed until the bridegroom cometh? The Son of God is bridegroom to every soul.

He that believeth not the Son, cannot have the Son in him. If a man does not believe, how can he house the spiritual light? As soon as he believes, he opens himself to the Son and the light streams in.

The Fourth Chapter

THE PURPOSE OF EXPERIENCE

BRETHREN, our prayer is that through communion one with the other, we arrive at deeper truth; this is our purpose in coming to talk with you – not that we, from the spirit, can teach you, but that together we may delve beneath the words of St John and find there a more profound truth than may appear on the surface. In contemplation and meditation you will always find more truth than our simple words can unfold.

We would speak now of the fourth chapter of the gospel, which tells the story, first, of the woman of Samaria. It is noticeable how often Jesus imparted his most profound teaching to women. His saying, 'I know to whom I am sent', indicates that he well knew to whom the Father Mother God intended him to speak. He withheld his deepest teaching from the high priests and rulers; nor did he always disclose the inner truths to his disciples – instead he often chose women, and, strange as it may seem to the worldly-minded, often women who were condemned by the world. For instance, he revealed the profound and glorious truth of the resurrection to Mary Magdalene – a woman looked down upon by many, yet Jesus chose her. And he chose also the woman at the well of Samaria – again, an apparently worldly woman. Why did Jesus select such women? No doubt it was because worldly experience can quicken understanding and develop sympathies. Suffering occasioned through the harshness of the world awakens sympathy and understanding in the soul. Do not neglect the duties of the world, for the development of the soul takes place through these experiences, and if the individual cares *only* for heavenly things without the balancing factor of worldly experience there must come a fall. We are touching here on the profound truth of the descent of the soul from heaven into matter. Through descent into the depths of matter the soul eventually becomes immortal.

You will notice that he first tested the people, both men and women, to whom he imparted deep spiritual truth. So he tested the woman of Samaria. He spoke to her of her worldly life, and of the number of husbands she had had. He did not consider these facts to be of any importance but he was impressed by the woman who said to him *I know that Messias cometh, which is called Christ: when he is come, he will tell us all things* (4 : 25) . . . the heavenly things, she meant, thus indicating that while her outlook might be worldly, she was also a soul prepared and ready. We should not conclude that a materially-minded man or woman necessarily lacks spiritual capacity, nor that only the saint is the one who can recognise truth intuitively or understand divine wisdom in a flash. A whole life can be spent in seclusion, in meditation and contemplation, and many incarnations seeking wisdom, but not until a certain thing happens within a man does the soul perceive truth, an awakening which comes through experience deep in earth, in matter.

At this juncture it will be helpful to read the story as told in the gospel.

(4 : 1–25) *When therefore the Lord knew how the Pharisees had heard that Jesus made and baptized more disciples than John (Though Jesus himself baptized not, but his disciples), he left Judaea, and departed again into Galilee.*

And he must needs go through Samaria. Then cometh he to a city of Samaria, which is called Sychar, near to the parcel of ground that Jacob gave to his son Joseph. Now Jacob's well was there. Jesus therefore, being wearied with his journey, sat thus on the well: and it was about the sixth hour. There cometh a woman of Samaria to draw water: Jesus saith unto her, Give me to drink. (For his disciples were gone away unto the city to buy meat.) Then saith the woman of Samaria unto him, How is it that thou, being a Jew, askest drink of me, which am a woman of Samaria? for the Jews have no dealings with the Samaritans.

Jesus answered and said unto her, If thou knewest the gift of God, and who it is that saith to thee, Give me to drink, thou wouldest have asked of him, and he would have given thee living water.

The woman saith unto him, Sir, thou hast nothing to draw with, and the well is deep: from whence then hast thou that living water? Art thou greater than our father Jacob, which gave us the well, and drank thereof himself, and his children, and his cattle?

Jesus answered and said unto her, Whosoever drinketh of this water shall thirst again: But whosoever drinketh of the water that I shall give him shall never thirst; but the water that I shall give him shall be in him a well of water springing up into everlasting life.

The woman saith unto him, Sir, give me this water, that I thirst not, neither come hither to draw.

Jesus saith unto her, Go, call thy husband, and come hither. The woman answered and said, I have no husband.

Jesus said unto her, Thou hast well said, I have no husband: For thou hast had five husbands; and he whom thou now hast is not thy husband: in that saidst thou truly.

The woman saith unto him, Sir, I perceive that thou art a prophet. Our fathers worshipped in this mountain, and ye say, that in Jerusalem is the place where men ought to worship.

Jesus saith unto her, Woman, believe me, the hour cometh when ye shall neither in this mountain, nor yet at Jerusalem, worship the Father. Ye worship ye know not what: we know what we worship: for salvation is of the Jews. But the hour cometh, and now is, when the true worshippers shall worship the Father in spirit and in truth: for the Father seeketh such to worship him. God is a Spirit: and they that worship him must worship him in spirit and in truth.

The woman saith unto him, I know that Messias cometh, which is called Christ: when he is come, he will tell us all things.

Here was the point (verse 25) at which the woman revealed to Jesus her readiness to receive the living water. Jesus always concerned himself with inner things and not with outer appearances, and when he said (having asked the woman to give him water from the well), *Whosoever drinketh of this water shall thirst again* (13), he was referring to the astral or desire body. Men and women are continually tempted to drink from the well of the world – which satisfies the desires of the astral body – rather than that of the spirit, of the spiritual life. If a man satisfies the desire body alone, then the desire body in time gets the upper hand, and however much he drinks from this well, his thirst will never be satisfied. The man who is ruled by his desire body clutches more and more to himself; he over-indulges the senses, yet still remains unsatisfied. He remains lonely and unhappy because he drinks only from the well of the world. But Jesus said that if the woman would ask him, he would give her water, the water of the spirit, which would satisfy her utterly, and quench her thirst forever.

In the East teachers urge their disciples to discipline the desire body by frugal living, by continued abstinence. The modern psychologist says, however, that if such desires and instincts are urgent in a man, let him satisfy and so get rid of them. Jesus indicated that neither is the true way. Man should not dwell upon his desires and appetites, either to fight or to indulge them, but rather transmute them by his aspirations. We do not suggest for instance that he should have long periods of fasting, but we do say he should be abstemious, and cultivate a taste for pure food, should take the foods of the earth in as natural a condition as possible but at the same time never fail to thank and glorify God for all the gifts life brings. Do not try to stamp out desire. Do not become an ascetic, but cultivate more refined tastes; and in accepting and enjoying what the world offers, try to purify and transmute the senses until you are no longer content with the water which quenches not your thirst; until, looking always to the divine spirit, Christ, for sustenance, your soul becomes purified because it is nourished by Christ's living water. *Whosoever drinketh of the water that I shall give him shall never thirst* (14) ... In this way carnal appetites and desires are overcome by the Christ grace and humility. Or, by thanking and glorifying God, you are transmuting the

33

particles of body and soul into the living body of the cosmic Christ.

(4 : 26–54) *Jesus saith unto her, I that speak unto thee am he. And upon this came his disciples, and marvelled that he talked with the woman, yet no man said, What seekest thou? or, Why talkest thou with her?*

The woman then left her water pot, and went her way into the city, and saith to the men, Come, see a man, which told me all things that ever I did: is not this the Christ? Then they went out of the city, and came unto him.

In the mean while his disciples prayed him, saying, Master, eat. But he said unto them, I have meat to eat that ye know not of. Therefore said the disciples one to another, Hath any man brought him aught to eat? Jesus saith unto them, My meat is to do the will of him that sent me, and to finish his work. Say not ye, There are yet four months, and then cometh harvest? Behold, I say unto you, Lift up your eyes, and look on the fields; for they are white already to harvest. And he that reapeth receiveth wages, and gathereth fruit unto life eternal: that both he that soweth and he that reapeth may rejoice together. And herein is that saying true, One soweth, and another reapeth. I sent you to reap that whereon ye bestowed no labour: other men laboured, and ye are entered into their labours.

And many of the Samaritans of that city believed on him for the saying of the woman, which testified, He told me all that ever I did. So when the Samaritans were come unto him, they besought him that he would tarry with them: and he abode there two days. And many more believed because of his own word; And said unto the woman, Now we believe, not because of thy saying; for we have heard him ourselves, and know that this is indeed the Christ, the Saviour of the world.

Now after two days he departed thence, and went into Galilee. For Jesus himself testified, that a prophet hath no honour in his own country. Then when he was come into Galilee, the Galilaeans received him, having seen all the things that he did at Jerusalem at the feast; for they also went unto the feast. So Jesus came again into

34

Cana of Galilee, where he made the water wine. And there was a certain nobleman, whose son was sick at Capernaum. When he heard that Jesus was come out of Judaea into Galilee, he went unto him, and besought him that he would come down, and heal his son: for he was at the point of death. Then said Jesus unto him, Except ye see signs and wonders, ye will not believe. The nobleman saith unto him, Sir, come down ere my child die. Jesus saith unto him, Go thy way; thy son liveth. And the man believed the word that Jesus had spoken unto him, and he went his way. And as he was now going down, his servants met him, and told him, saying, Thy son liveth. Then inquired he of them the hour when he began to amend. And they said unto him, Yesterday at the seventh hour the fever left him. So the father knew that it was at the same hour, in the which Jesus said unto him, Thy son liveth: and himself believed, and his whole house. This is again the second miracle that Jesus did, when he was come out of Judaea into Galilee.

My meat is to do the will of him that sent me (34). This means that loving action was the food; it was food to him, to give, in action. Jesus spoke of his food being the will to action. This is important, for it is cosmic law that in giving you receive, and if you receive, you must always give forth again. It was meat to Jesus to *live* the Word of God by serving those to whom he had been sent by his Father.

Here we would interpolate that it is shown again and again in the gospel that the truths of reincarnation and karma were known by Jesus; indeed, without knowledge of reincarnation we cannot fully understand the meaning underlying his teachings. For instance, when referring to certain people he indicated that he knew to whom he had been sent because he had power to see their past lives. He could see the karma, both good and ill, which their souls had gathered, and knew what their future would bring because of what had happened in their past. He speaks of sowing and reaping and infers that the harvest of seed sown in one lifetime was not usually reaped in the same life. Thus a teacher may broadcast his 'seed', but the harvest may not appear until several incarnations later. The sower and the reaper are not necessarily the same, for while, to some, the truth a teacher imparts may be new, others may already have had truth implanted in them in the past, and for them in the present incarnation, the fields may be white unto harvest. Or in other words there may be many prepared to follow their master. When the fields whiten the master comes, and recognising his own, gathers the harvest home.

It is like the parable of the sower – another example of seeds that, although sown, do not grow immediately. Those who have listened to truth disperse. No more is heard of them in that particular incarnation, but some day the fields will become ready for harvesting. For instance (39–42) we are told that many of the Samaritans believed, not because of any demonstration of psychic power, but because, on hearing the living word from the Master, their inner self told them that he spoke truth and they accepted him.

In verse 21, when Jesus spoke of worship – *The hour cometh ... when ye shall neither in this mountain, nor yet at Jerusalem, worship the Father* – he was indicating that only in the temple within man can the real worship take place; and that when the woman had undergone the initiation that was at hand for her, her whole life would express itself in worship.

They that worship him must worship him in spirit and in truth (24) – worship Him, that is, not in any outer temple, but in the living temple of their own being; worship Him by living purely, healthily, naturally.

If only man could understand the holiness of his own body instead of regarding it as something to be overworked, indulged or neglected! If only man would grow to reverence his body and learn to breathe in the life forces of God, to cleanse the body with pure water, to eat pure fruits of the earth and drink pure waters from the spring! If only he would learn to hold his body upright, poised and graceful, with feet planted firmly and the whole being erect, and let the light of the Sun pour into his heart thus glorifying God! This indeed is to eat the food and drink the living waters of Christ. Did not Jesus tell the woman at the well that she must *ask* for the living water – thus indicating to man the importance of prayer. The soul must aspire, must in all earnestness and truth pray: 'O, may I be blessed in my service, blessed in my actions, blessed with the grace of Thy life quickening in this temple of Thy creation, my body. May I so live that my every deed is a blessing and a sacrament. May I not desecrate Thy temple.'

The last verses of the chapter, recording the healing of the son of the nobleman who sought the help of Jesus, provide a clear demonstration of healing at a distance. All healing is psychic, because sickness of the body is the result of dis-ease in the soul or psyche. You may challenge this statement but we deal with this subject again later and we think you will find that what we have said is true.

The Fifth Chapter

HEALING IN SPIRIT

TRUTH must be sought not merely with the mind but is found as an answering note, in the depths of your being, to the vibrations of the Logos. Our words may help to stimulate a certain response in you, but if you would gain wisdom and realisation, you must learn to listen inwardly to the voice which speaks in your innermost. Don't merely read the words, but try to feel and respond to the influence of heavenly messengers who descend through the spheres to come close and inspire humanity. These heavenly messengers pour upon you the radiance of their love, and their light permeates the very atoms of your physical, mental, astral and spiritual vehicles, quickening your consciousness to a realisation of the heavenly life. Their influence can also affect you unconsciously, in that in your everyday life you act spontaneously in response to the good stimulus. Kindness, service, love, becomes instinctive and habitual, as in the saints, in whom we find a light glowing, a glory ever shining.

The true man rings true not because of himself, 'not in his own name', but because he is unaware of anything but the divine. Living, moving and having his being in God, he is continually receiving divine love. Living in the light, the light shines through him.

The fifth chapter of the gospel, on which we now embark, is concerned to a great extent with healing. Before examining it in greater detail we should like to talk generally on the subject of psychic or soul healing. You will remember we stated that all sickness was traceable to the psyche; because of this certain herbs and medicines can be used, which, by affecting the psyche, will prepare the way for the reception of the true healing power of God; they contain elements which minister to the psychic as well as to the physical body. It is through the psyche, or psychic body that healing of the physical body takes place.

In the chapter which follows we shall find a reference to the disturbing of the waters of the pool called Bethesda. When the waters were ruffled the sick could plunge in and receive healing, the narrative states. We interpret this to mean that the psyche of the man had first to be prepared.

Having said that disease is traceable either to the psyche or to the subconscious (or to what might be better described as the preconsciousness of man), we would add that some illness is also due to unrecognised obsession. The ancient races were aware that the subconscious mind was the seat of many diseases. The so-called witch doctor, who possessed a specialised knowledge, would work on the subconscious of the patient and by his treatment release the patient from certain inhibitions and dis-ease. There were certain conditions however which could not be accounted for in this manner. So also does the modern psychologist find himself helpless on occasion. If he could only recognise the laws of reincarnation and karma he would see that many conditions are due not only to subconscious memories harboured by the physical body, but also to soul-memories.

For instance, long ages past a man may have created a certain condition through ill deeds, ill thoughts, or through lust for power; perhaps, because of this, certain so-called dark forces may have become attached to him. He may have attracted to himself elementals which, strange as it may seem, have a very long life. Such past conditions – or what we will call preconscious states – may return to the soul when it reincarnates, so that the soul enters upon the 'judgment' referred to in this chapter. The evils attracted to and stored up in the man's aura return in subsequent incarnations, and then they have to be faced, they must be expiated.

It has been said that the elemental forms which man has created for himself can penetrate and attach themselves to the aura and can sometimes be seen by an advanced clairvoyant. These attachments, working through the psyche, ultimately reach the physical body, to manifest as a disease; or their influence can even bring about an accident. There is no such thing as chance or mischance. Once the divine law of life is understood it is seen that all things originate from a cause which lies deeper than mere carelessness or ignorance.

Certain diseases seem to be incurable, and for no apparent reason the patient slips through the doctor's hands; this means that specific conditions brought over from the past are working themselves out to their conclusion. Then they are finished with, expiated. Man may have created these elemental forms through his own passion, greed or desire for power over his fellow men; indeed, everything which opposes pure love and true brotherhood is of the shadow. If these elementals are not expunged in one incarnation they wait until the next incarnation, and so on – *unto the third and fourth generation* (or incarnation) (Exod. 20:5). The true healer should remember that it may not always be right for healing of the body to take place – that sometimes, through the suffering and death of the body, indescribable good is coming to the soul. If people could only recognise the wise and beautiful law of the Father Mother God which guides all human life, how much happier they would be! For then they would be able truly to say, 'Thy will be done'.

These words do not imply however that we should sit down and let God wait on us. No, they mean that having done our best according to our understanding, having prepared in all ways for divine love to work in us, then we must rest in God's love. God's will is wise and, above all, loving; it is also exact and perfect law. Once the soul of man can respond in absolute purity to the love or the life of God, his body will be suddenly and completely healed by the true spiritual healing. Such deep healing is rare indeed, for few are ready to make so complete a surrender to the love of God. God *is* life. It is not enough to say 'I believe in God's love', for truly the soul must *become* divine love, which is rare. If you study the lives of the saints and that of Jesus above all, you will see the true meaning of the word love; you will see the constant outflowing of this true spirit of love – shall we call it, this gentle Jesus? We like that expression, which conveys so clearly and simply the meaning of love. *Gentle* Jesus – who withheld nothing, but gave continually; who poured forth love to all creatures, to all men, from the highest to the humblest. Every fine and noble quality you can name can be expressed through the spirit in man, as it is continually being expressed by the cosmic law which governs all life. Even what is miscalled evil is used as a working tool by God to unearth treasure – used first to destroy, to break down, then to rebuild and recreate.

Psychic power, psychic healing, works through the psyche to the physical body. Yet Jesus showed there was a better method. Jesus healed through his pure outpouring of love – love was the key, love was the secret, but such a love as is rarely experienced or understood by men on earth. Jesus, or the Christ in him, had reached so complete an at-one-ment with the Father that he received God's life-force without hindrance. Life is love. He was able not only to transmit such love, but could so quicken the vibration of his patient that the sick soul was raised up and responded to divine love. Of himself, the patient might fail; but with the help of so pure and perfect a man as Christ Jesus, he was able to respond to the divine power which restored him.

Now let us study the fifth chapter.

(5 : 1–9) *After this there was a feast of the Jews; and Jesus went up to Jerusalem. Now there is at Jerusalem by the sheep market a pool, which is called in the Hebrew tongue Bethesda, having five porches. In these lay a great multitude of impotent folk, of blind, halt, withered, waiting for the moving of the water. For an angel went down at a certain season into the pool, and troubled the water: whosoever then first after the troubling of the water stepped in was made whole of whatsoever disease he had. And a certain man was there, which had an infirmity thirty and eight years. When Jesus saw him lie, and knew that he had been now a long time in that case, he saith unto him, Wilt thou be made whole? The impotent man answered him, Sir, I have no man, when the water is troubled, to put me into the pool: but while I am coming, another steppeth down*

before me. Jesus saith unto him, Rise, take up thy bed, and walk. And immediately the man was made whole, and took up his bed, and walked: and on the same day was the sabbath.

An interesting point here is the angel who disturbed the waters. Angels of healing are always present during what is called spiritual healing. In an absent healing group* sitters prepare themselves and call upon the angels of healing, the angels of Christ; the angels draw near and, as the bible says, 'trouble the waters'. In other words they stir the *soul* of the patient to respond to the healing ray.

You ask if music or colour can also affect the psyche? Yes, the vibrations of sound and light can stimulate the psychic centres so that the soul can receive healing. So also can certain herbs and minerals 'trouble the waters', or prepare the soul body or psyche.

We draw your attention to the completeness of this healing, *Rise, take up thy bed, and walk* (8). The command of the Father uttered through the Son; the command of the Father to the Son within, the Son who is in the patient. Rise! – and the Christ spirit forthwith arose. The cry was to the sleeping Christ in the soul of that sick man. 'Rise brother, take up thy bed and walk. Hear the call of Christ, Son of God. Do not cease from effort until the goal of spiritual liberation be reached . . . attain spiritual vision, spiritual emancipation!' The challenge was to the dormant spirit to wake from sleep. Take up thy bed and walk – or, in other words, be active to express thyself through this man.

(5:10–18) *The Jews therefore said unto him that was cured, It is the sabbath day: it is not lawful for thee to carry thy bed. He answered them, He that made me whole, the same said unto me, Take up thy bed, and walk. Then asked they him, What man is that which said unto thee, Take up thy bed, and walk? And he that was healed wist not who it was: for Jesus had conveyed himself away, a*

* White Eagle is here referring to absent healing as practised in the White Eagle Lodge.

multitude being in that place. Afterward Jesus findeth him in the temple, and said unto him, Behold, thou art made whole: sin no more, lest a worse thing come unto thee. The man departed, and told the Jews that it was Jesus, which had made him whole. And therefore did the Jews persecute Jesus, and sought to slay him, because he had done these things on the sabbath day. But Jesus answered them, My Father worketh hitherto, and I work. Therefore the Jews sought the more to kill him, because he not only had broken the sabbath, but said also that God was his Father, making himself equal with God.

What an issue the Jews made of Jesus healing on the sabbath! Their concern was with the fulfilling of the letter of the law, rather than the spirit. Jesus showed that it mattered nothing; and that the temple of God was neither built of stone nor bricks but was the consciousness of man when he worships God. Jesus recognised the innermost of man's being as the true temple of worship. The 'sabbath day' is every day during which man expresses only love and does the will of his Father. Any day is a sabbath to the man expressing God.

Afterward Jesus findeth him in the temple, and said unto him, Behold, thou art made whole: sin no more, lest a worse thing come unto thee (14). Do you not see that when Jesus by a miracle healed a sick or crippled body, such a cure might last only for the span of the one lifetime if the man's *soul* failed to respond? But if the soul quickened to divine love the cure could be for eternity, for the karma would be transmuted. Without this transmutation by love the reincarnating soul will be confronted by its karma in succeeding lives. Note how Jesus, by his act, was affecting the karma of those whom he had healed. Even up to the crucifixion, he performed miracles, acted with supreme compassion and love, drawing to himself the karma of those he saved. In this case the patient was indebted to Jesus for his healing; therefore new karma was created, but Jesus would not exact payment. And so Jesus went about helping souls to become regenerated, to transmute their karma. Instead of demanding an eye for an eye, Jesus gave back love and thus helped the person concerned to expiate past karma.

If you can return love instead of resentment and hate to anyone who injures you, you are released from the bondage of your karma with that one, and releasing him. By so doing Jesus also affected the karma of many souls while on his mission. He has been affecting the karma of the world ever since; for world karma is being gradually changed through the love of Christ: this is the transmutation of karma through love.

(5 : 19–20) *Then answered Jesus and said unto them, Verily, verily, I say unto you, The Son can do nothing of himself, but what he seeth the Father do: for what things soever he doeth, these also doeth the Son likewise. For the Father loveth the Son, and sheweth him all things that himself doeth: and he will shew him greater works than these, that ye may marvel.*

The Son can do nothing of himself, but what he sees the Father do. The Son, the Christ child, dwells in man but can do nothing of itself, only when he can respond to the will of the Father. What the glory of the Son, shining through Jesus, accomplished, will in due course be accomplished through all God's children when they have fulfilled the requirements of the spiritual law which enable so-called miracles to take place. The Christ in the individual, when the man sees, when he comprehends and responds, then he will do the will of the Father through him and grow towards God.

(5 : 21–22) *For as the Father raiseth up the dead, and quickeneth them; even so the Son quickeneth whom he will. For the Father judgeth no man, but hath committed all judgment unto the Son.*

God judgeth no man, but God's laws are nevertheless inevitable and immutable. God does not judge, but surrenders judgment to the Son.

That Son is in man, and man will eventually judge himself.

We are told that man's soul will come before the judgment seat, before the throne of God. This outmoded and orthodox teaching nevertheless contains fundamental truth, for when the soul ultimately stands before the glory of the light it cannot help but judge itself. Not until the soul can see itself, judge itself, can it make progress. In incarnation after incarnation the same lessons come forward; time after time they are put aside until at some crucial moment the soul sees itself revealed as it truly is. It knows itself – 'man know thyself' – and judges itself. In the ancient mystery schools the neophyte was taken before a magic mirror, in which he saw himself, his true inner self, reflected. And he, the son in him, judged himself.*

There is another interpretation. The life of the Father is love; and by the life of the Father passing into the Son, the Son also becomes pure and absolute love. Now, when a man is thus filled with God's life or love, he no longer judges by the law of earth but by the law of heaven. His judgment is then that of love. But when love judges there can be no erroneous judgment. Only absolute love can judge aright. Can you not see? Love only can give power to judge or discriminate wisely.

(5 : 23) *That all men should honour the Son, even as they honour the Father. He that honoureth not the Son honoureth not the Father which hath sent him.*

My brethren, a wonderful truth is embodied in these words. We will try to put it as simply as possible. To honour the Son is to honour the Christ revealed to us as the Son of God through Jesus. We honour, we adore him . . . but our brother man by our side we neither honour, nor serve, indeed, we may condemn him. Nevertheless Jesus distinctly tells his hearers to honour the Son; for if you do not, how can you honour the God who sent him? The Son cometh from the Father, and that Son is your brother man, for the Son lives in your brother. When this is realised we shall begin to see the dawn of the brotherhood of man. That every man should honour his brother – this is the perfect teaching of brotherhood.

* See Appendix, p. 187, 'Judgment'.

(5 : 24–29) *Verily, verily, I say unto you, He that heareth my word, and believeth on him that sent me, hath everlasting life, and shall not come into condemnation; but is passed from death unto life. Verily, verily, I say unto you, The hour is coming, and now is, when the dead shall hear the voice of the Son of God; and they that hear shall live. For as the Father hath life in himself; so hath he given to the Son to have life in himself; And hath given him authority to execute judgment also, because he is the Son of man. Marvel not at this; for the hour is coming in the which all that are in the graves shall hear his voice, and shall come forth; they that have done good, unto the resurrection of life; and they that have done evil, unto the resurrection of damnation.*

The Master, when speaking of the resurrection of life, said in effect, 'He that has done good will arise from the dead'. This was once thought to mean that the bodies of the good would arise from their graves, but we read into the Master's words that when he refers to the soul rising to eternal life, he means that the soul will become so purified and quickened that it need not reincarnate again, and is thus raised from death into glory. The soul condemned to the 'resurrection of damnation' (we think the translation somewhat overstresses the case) means that the soul will have to reincarnate, will have to undergo further periods of imprisonment in flesh, until all lessons have been learned, and the soul at last inherits eternal life. You will find a similar truth expressed in the teachings of the Lord Buddha. The Buddhist seeks release from the round of rebirth and endeavours so to live as to avoid creating fresh karma to bind him to this wheel.

(5 : 30–40) *I can of mine own self do nothing: as I hear, I judge: and my judgment is just; because I seek not mine own will, but the will of the Father which hath sent me. If I bear witness of myself, my witness is not true. There is another that beareth witness of me, and I know that the witness which he witnesseth of me is true. Ye sent unto John, and he bare witness unto the truth. But I receive not testimony from man; but these things I say, that ye might be saved. He was a burning and a shining light: and ye were willing for a*

season to rejoice in his light. But I have greater witness than that of John: for the works which the Father hath given me to finish, the same works that I do, bear witness of me, that the Father hath sent me. And the Father himself, which hath sent me, hath borne witness of me. Ye have neither heard his voice at any time, nor seen his shape. And ye have not his word abiding in you: for whom he hath sent, him ye believe not. Search the scriptures: for in them ye think ye have eternal life; and they are they which testify of me. And ye will not come to me, that ye might have life.

John was a light (as all wise men are illumined) but the Son of man must follow his own light, which is more brilliant than any which can come from another. You may look upon a teacher and see in him a spiritual radiance, but not so great a radiance as that light of the Father Mother in the Christ-child, which is the greater light, which lighteth every man. Not the light from another soul, however good, but the light from the Son within, that is the way, the truth and the life. That is why we say, do not do what *we* tell you, do not depend upon *us*, but follow the light in your own heart. Your own response to the Logos will be your true light.

(5 : 41–47) *I receive not honour from men. But I know you, that ye have not the love of God in you. I am come in my Father's name, and ye receive me not: if another shall come in his own name, him ye will receive. How can ye believe, which receive honour one of another, and seek not the honour that cometh from God only? Do not think that I will accuse you to the Father: there is one that accuseth you, even Moses, in whom ye trust. For had ye believed Moses, ye would have believed me: for he wrote of me. But if ye believe not his writings, how shall ye believe my words?*

He that comes in the name of the Father remains meek and often lives humbly, making no claims. The world receives him not. But the man who comes in his own name, with much advertisement, the world will accept. But, my brethren, it is the sweet inner love of the Son for which we must look in our brother, and nothing else. Name, position, wealth, are as nothing compared to the light of the Son within. This it is for which we must search in our brother, this it is which we must learn to recognise, and to which we must respond.

Throughout these verses the Master Jesus is speaking of eternal reality and truth and is endeavouring to stimulate in his hearers a response to the Logos, to the truth which has been from the beginning and which has been embodied in all the teachings of the mystery schools. Jesus spoke of Moses as one who had known the truth of the Ancient Wisdom . . . *had ye believed Moses, ye would have believed me* (46). When a man responds to the voice of God within him he knows truth. He doesn't need convincing, he needs no argument. Truth is in him, and quickens and brings him to life. It raises him from death to life. All this was spoken by the Son of the Father, by the true light which we call Christ, which shone through Jesus – the light which is of the Father, and which can come into man's being as a result of his response to the vibration of the Logos.

The will of your Father Mother is that you should love one another. To do the will of God is to love, and in loving and obeying His will and commandment, ye shall know truth. Truth shall free you from all bondage, physical, mental and astral, and from desire, ill-health, sorrow and karma. It will free you from karma and rebirth. The truth of the Christ within shall liberate the soul to eternal freedom.

Let us thank God, my brethren, for all the love, truth and happiness which we feel. Lacking God's love we are nothing. Without this spirit of the Father Mother we are nothing. Any happiness you feel, any joy which comes, my children, is the result of your own acceptance of God and the grand company of angels and men.

Father Mother God, we thank Thee; we thank Thee for this further opportunity to learn from Thee. We thank Thee for love and light within our being. Do with us as Thou wilt; Thy will be done in us. For Thou art all wisdom and all love, and Thou wilt give us health, holiness, perfection, happiness.

The Sixth Chapter

THE BREAD OF LIFE

THE MYSTICAL teaching to be found in the gospel of St John, once it is understood, contains everything that man needs for his spiritual life. So much however remains unexplained in the Christian teaching. The words of Jesus are usually interpreted on the material plane, but the student of spiritual truth recognises that all such teaching holds a threefold meaning, can be interpreted at three levels. To illustrate this: the sixth chapter of St John is usually interpreted at the physical level, but it also refers to the mental plane, and then distinguishes between the mental and the spiritual. The jewel of truth has many facets, all the facets being complementary one to the other, no one facet containing the whole truth; through each shines a ray of truth and all take their illumination from the centre of the jewel. The core of the whole lies in its spiritual meaning.

People frequently make the mistake of separating the various aspects of truth; they try to divorce the material from the spiritual. This is incorrect – you must look upon life as a whole, recognising the purpose and value of every aspect and harmonising all into one perfect expression of truth. You do not say, 'My hands have nothing to do with my feet – I cannot use my hands to walk with, therefore I will discard them'. Your hands have work which only they can perform; your feet also have their function. So it is with all the planes of being, all aspects of truth. The physical has its work and purpose, otherwise God would not have created it, and the material life too has its place in the development of man. We cannot cast aside material duties, for we are here on earth to master matter, and the soul who neglects to watch where it is going has a tumble and suffers a few cuts and bruises. There must be a harmonious balance between all planes of being. Harmony, balance, this is the object of life.

49

In a few moments we shall read the stories of the feeding of the five thousand, and of Jesus walking upon the water. Now, remember what we have said about the interpretation of truth at different levels; so-called miracles can and do take place on the physical and material plane. 'Miracle' is a word used to describe a happening outside the working of known physical law; but truly, a miracle is the result of the natural outworking of divine law in a physical state.

On this occasion there were only two small fishes and five loaves with which to feed the multitude. When these had been blessed by the Master and distributed amongst the five thousand, there proved sufficient for all, and no less than twelve baskets of fragments remained uneaten, the twelve baskets containing more food than there was at the beginning. Is it possible that such a miracle could really take place? Yes, because the Master understood spiritual law. He was a master of matter, and knew how to use the creative power within him to manipulate material atoms. By a process of raising the consciousness, such a creative act can take place; the additional food can be materialised from the universal substance of life by one who is a master, a master of all matter. All our needs can be supplied once we understand the power of love.

At the same time, there is another interpretation of this miracle. We usually read that Jesus 'went up into a mountain to pray'; and often he took his disciples with him. This means that Jesus raised his consciousness and the consciousness of his disciples to a higher level – he 'went up into a mountain'.

We too can do this, in a lesser degree; when we meditate, our first aim is to climb away from earthliness. We go up, as it were, into a mountain; and when we are set, the master comes. We have first to be raised above the material things, to reach heavenwards, and in that state of consciousness we have experiences which we are quite unable to explain or speak of afterwards, for no words will clothe what we have seen.

After they had been up into a mountain of prayer, of aspiration, Jesus beheld a great company gathered around him. Could that company have been discarnate? We think that this was a multitude of men and women hungry for truth. Jesus, perceiving this, started to talk to them; by his own love and spiritual power he raised their vibrations, but still they hungered, still there was that in them which yearned for the bread of life, for a spiritual food. Then Jesus turned to the disciples and asked if there were anything with which they could be fed. He knew the answer, but was testing them. One replied, *There is a lad here, which hath five barley loaves, and two small fishes: but what are they among so many?* (9).

Consider the symbolism of the loaves and fishes. Can we read into the episode that the Master himself, in his incarnation as Jesus of Nazareth, symbolised the two fishes and the barley loaves – that he was the food which the people needed? Remember, he was the great teacher of the Piscean Age, an age symbolised by the fishes. The barley loaves symbolise the true bread of life, the life-giving bread. Jesus then gave himself to God, or called down a blessing upon this food. In other words he surrendered himself to the divine and perfect life; the power descended upon him, and the food, the living food of truth, through him was distributed to all. He gave himself in service to the multitude. Now there is a law about spiritual giving. You cannot give spiritually, without receiving something in return. If you are observant, you will notice that amongst spiritual workers the more that is poured out in the true spirit, the more is received. Jesus gave so much of his spiritual self that when all had been eaten, all the spiritual food had been absorbed, the disciples packed twelve baskets with that which was left. How wonderful that with this spiritual outpouring there remains more than enough for all, and the disciples are able to fill their baskets with the fragments which the multitudes are unable to assimilate. The supply of spiritual truth, spiritual power, is inexhaustible.

Jesus later speaks of the 'bread of life'. He speaks of the Father God (we would rather use the term the 'Father Mother' God, for it is impossible to separate the two), saying in effect, 'Thou, O God, art the true bread of life, and Thou hast given

Thy spirit to Thy Son. Thy Son partakes of Thy spirit; therefore the Father and the Son are One, Father Mother Son, the one, holy, perfect, blessed Trinity of life. Because the spirit of my Father Mother abides in me, I am that bread. Not the words that I speak, but the power which goes forth from me is the bread of life for all men. Take and eat; this is my body'.

But we go further, for we see the body of the Cosmic Christ permeating all life from the celestial to the physical; for mother earth herself, who is the producer of the physical bread of life, is impregnated with the light, the body of Christ. Father Mother God, Thou givest sustenance for body, mind and spirit, sufficient for every plane of our being!

Jesus goes on to say that the manna which Moses gave to the people was not the bread from heaven. That manna which fell to feed the children of Israel in the wilderness was food for the mind, not the spirit. Many people, particularly in this age, are searching for such manna, a mental food, thinking it to be bread from heaven, and becoming absorbed in intricate mental exercises which, while interesting and entertaining, still leave the spirit hungry. The manna, which means the mind, the attributes of the mental plane, satisfied the Israelites for the moment. But Jesus emphasises that this is not the true bread. *I am the bread of life* (35) . . . 'I AM the bread of life' – the true bread of life is the pure spirit of God, the spirit of Christ, which transcends all mental limitations and which overflows with love. Even interpreted purely as a physical miracle, you will recognise in the story of the feeding of the five thousand Jesus' great love for the people and his understanding of their needs and feelings. He could enter into the soul of each one, feeling the hunger and longing of each one in himself.

We would like you now to read the chapter carefully and interpret what you read for yourself in the light of our suggestions. Again we say, brethren, follow the inner light, be your own interpreter; let the Christ illumine your minds, and you will probably receive a great deal more than we ourselves can reveal.

(6 : 1–26) *After these things Jesus went over the sea of Galilee, which is the sea of Tiberias. And a great multitude followed him, because they saw his miracles which he did on them that were diseased. And Jesus went up into a mountain, and there he sat with his disciples. And the passover, a feast of the Jews, was nigh. When Jesus then lifted up his eyes, and saw a great company come unto him, he saith unto Philip, Whence shall we buy bread, that these may eat? And this he said to prove him: for he himself knew what he would do.*

Philip answered him, Two hundred pennyworth of bread is not sufficient for them, that every one of them may take a little. One of his disciples, Andrew, Simon Peter's brother, saith unto him, There is a lad here, which hath five barley loaves, and two small fishes: but what are they among so many? And Jesus said, Make the men sit down.

Now there was much grass in the place. So the men sat down, in number about five thousand. And Jesus took the loaves: and when he had given thanks, he distributed to the disciples, and the disciples to them that were set down; and likewise of the fishes as much as they would. When they were filled, he said unto his disciples, Gather up the fragments that remain, that nothing be lost. Therefore, they gathered them together, and filled twelve baskets with the fragments of the five barley loaves, which remained over and above unto them that had eaten. Then those men, when they had seen the miracle that Jesus did, said, This is of a truth that prophet that should come into the world.

When Jesus therefore perceived that they would come and take him by force, to make him a king, he departed again into a mountain himself alone. And when even was now come, his disciples went down unto the sea. And entered into a ship, and went over the sea toward Capernaum. And it was now dark, and Jesus was not come to them. And the sea arose by reason of a great wind that blew. So when they had rowed about five and twenty or thirty furlongs, they see Jesus walking on the sea, and drawing nigh unto the ship: and they were afraid.

But he saith unto them, It is I; be not afraid. Then they willingly received him into the ship: and immediately the ship was at the land whither they went.

The day following, when the people which stood on the other side of the sea saw that there was none other boat there, save that one whereinto his disciples were entered, and that Jesus went not with his disciples into the boat, but that his disciples were gone away alone; (Howbeit there came other boats from Tiberias nigh unto the place where they did eat bread, after that the Lord had given thanks:) When the people therefore saw that Jesus was not there, neither his disciples, they also took shipping, and came to Capernaum, seeking for Jesus. And when they had found him on the other side of the sea, they said unto him, Rabbi, when camest thou hither? Jesus answered them and said, Verily, verily, I say unto you, Ye seek me, not because ye saw the miracles, but because ye did eat of the loaves, and were filled.

This last saying is a most important one, and contains the key to the whole chapter. You notice that Jesus said it was because they ate the bread; in other words, because his hearers had absorbed from Jesus the divine spirit, the glorious light which went forth from him, that they were raised, initiated into the higher life. It is not the beholding of miracles which produces the effect, but the entering into the inner chamber and feeling the presence of the Christ. As you absorb into you His being, you are eating the very bread of life, you commune with Him. Not the words, not the miracles at which you marvel, but the bread of life which you absorb, the presence, the spirit, the blessing of the Master – this is communion.

The incident of Jesus walking on the water demonstrated that he was above conflict arising from the emotional and lower mental planes. The Master Jesus walked upon the waves. And when the disciples took him into their storm-tossed boat, the seas subsided and the ship reached the haven whither they desired to go. In other words, as soon as emotions are brought under control – as soon as you, the disciples, accept and draw the Christ into your frail craft, you are immediately out of danger, you are in port. All is well. Try to remember that.

(6 : 27–35) Labour not for the meat which perisheth, but for that meat which endureth unto everlasting life, which the Son of man shall give unto you: for him hath God the Father sealed. Then said they unto him, What shall we do that we might work the works of God?

Jesus answered and said unto them, This is the work of God, that ye believe on him whom he hath sent. They said therefore unto him, What sign shewest thou then, that we may see, and believe thee? what dost thou work? Our fathers did eat manna in the desert; as it is written, He gave them bread from heaven to eat.

Then said Jesus unto them, Verily, verily, I say unto you, Moses gave you not that bread from heaven; but my Father giveth you the true bread from heaven. For the bread of God is he which cometh down from heaven, and giveth life unto the world.

Then said they unto him, Lord, evermore give us this bread. And Jesus said unto them, I am the bread of life: he that cometh to me shall never hunger; and he that believeth on me shall never thirst.

(The remaining verses of this chapter continue this theme.)

He that believeth on me has been interpreted as a question of faith, 'Have faith! Believe on me!' But the words mean more than belief in the ordinary sense; to believe in Jesus the Christ means to absorb his life, and to *live* his life; to live according to his pattern. This is true believing.

To believe in me, the 'I AM', means to become so guided, so infused with the gentle life, the gentle love, that we become like Christ. Believing is *becoming* the light, the love, the wisdom, the tenderness, the justice and the truth of Christ; it is knowing the power of the Christ within.

One or two further points arise. You remember Jesus saying on another occasion (Mt. 5 : 8) that the pure in heart would see God. In this chapter, he says that only those who have seen God can recognise in him (Jesus) the Son of God – only the simple, the childlike, the pure. Another interpretation of this passage we suggest concerns the symbolic eating of the body and the drinking of the blood of Jesus. Here we can perceive the teaching of brotherhood in its widest sense of brotherhood of the spirit. Here every man partakes of the body and the blood (the spiritual life) of his brother man; and thus feels, enters into, his experiences, his emotions, his sorrows and aspirations. Brotherhood is the perfect way of life; we can think of nothing higher than true brotherhood. Jesus said, *Love one another* (Jn. 15 : 12); and again *Love the Lord thy God with all thy heart, and with all thy soul, and with all thy mind* (Mt. 22:37). By this he meant giving forth true brotherly love to all men – not to the few, not merely to those you like – but to everyone, sharing with them the bread and the wine of the spirit.

Jesus again refers to signs and wonders as meaning little or nothing. Manna does not give men eternal life. They cannot receive the true life through the mind or intellect alone, but only through love of Christ in their hearts. The divine fire of eternal life springs from the heart, where Christ dwells.

The Seventh Chapter

DISCERNING TRUE VALUES

A FREQUENTLY recurring fairy tale tells the story of a prince who sets forth upon a quest which in the end brings him the hand of a beautiful princess. He is usually warned at the start of the dangers he will encounter; nevertheless he is undaunted and declares that he will attain his goal. After many vicissitudes he does reach the castle and finds and weds the princess of his dreams. This union is symbolical of the soul's union with the higher self, reunion with the beloved. It is the story of the path of every man.

But what has this fairy story of the soul's quest to do with the seventh chapter of the gospel of St John? This, that Jesus tells his disciples the same story in a different form. We have all been sent forth from the heart of our Father Mother God on a quest, and sometimes we suffer deeply as we travel the road. As soon as the soul sets forth consciously upon its spiritual quest it becomes aware of two distinct paths, that of the worldly-wise man, and that of the Godly-wise man. This world is only too ready to condemn, to ridicule, and to tempt poor Christian [as in Bunyan's PILGRIM'S PROGRESS] to stray from his path.

As we read this chapter, you will observe a note of controversy, of unbelief, for the Scribes and Pharisees question the validity of the teachings of Jesus. (These were the intellectuals of that day, and indeed of all time, for Scribes and Pharisees will always exist, it is a stage of development through which men go.) *And the Jews marvelled, saying, How knoweth this man letters, having never learned?* (15). This is ever the response of the worldly mind. They did not understand that there exists in the universe a deep well of truth which the soul can touch, which can be drawn upon in deep meditation by the soul who has reached a state of true humility, by the soul who knows that all

57

truth, all goodness, comes from God. Jesus said, *There is none good but one, that is God* (Mt. 19 : 17). Goodness originates from God; the illumined soul is aware that any wisdom it possesses is not of itself, but flows from the stream of truth which is God, comes from the mind of God – the mind of God, not the mind of self.

How is this state of reception to truth from the universal realms of wisdom to be attained? Through constant aspiration, through sincerity of life and one-pointedness: we mean by this that the soul, having once become aware that it is on a quest searching for a treasure of priceless worth, will endeavour to attune itself to the spirit, and to discriminate, to discern the spiritual essence underlying every manifestation and happening in life.

The truly great recognise and discern instantly the true way of life as apart from the false, the true way in which all life's values are recognised as spiritual. The average man judges things according to their market price, mostly by outward appearances. He sees shining gold and thinks this will satisfy him forever. He seizes gold, locks it away, and lives and dies safeguarding a worthless prize. Such is mortal man's valuation of life. But the man of God values all things by their spiritual worth.

At times it is difficult to discriminate between the worthless and the worthwhile. When at last you are certain of your path and your values begin to change you may find that you are resented; it seems that sometimes the spiritual influence brings an unconscious reaction from the worldly, and there is resentment and difficulty even though people are kind and well-meaning. Those who have had some vision of the true spiritual path are usually eager to share it with others; some, however, are over-eager, over-enthusiastic, and unwise. The man of God, after a little experience, learns to keep very quiet and endeavours to help only by giving kindliness and love to his fellows.

The Master was well aware of the existence of the worldly-wise man. In this chapter we shall find that Jesus was speaking the whole time of the inner life. The Scribes and Pharisees and many of his followers, and indeed some of his disciples, were puzzled; they thought he was deceiving them, and proved only too ready to stir up strife and resentment against Jesus. So, when the feast of the Jews came, Jesus sent his disciples to the Temple saying he was not yet ready to come. Yet he went quietly, on his own.

What can we read from this? Jesus withdrew from his companions into the inner planes for communion, for vision, even as you yourselves enter into meditation, withdrawing from the outer world, yet retaining your full consciousness; in this state a master is unlimited by time and space and able to travel in the soul body where he will. We think then, that Jesus entered into a state of meditation, and in that state went to the feast to see what was taking place. The disciples and the Jews were puzzled; they knew he was present, somewhere. They felt fear and resentment because they could neither see nor touch him.

Later Jesus speaks of going to some place whither his disciples could not follow. The Jews were irritated at this and said, *Whither will he go, that we shall not find him?* (35). Where Jesus went was beyond all intellectual comprehension, beyond all religious teaching and knowledge of the day. Jesus was going to be reunited with his beloved in that golden castle far-removed. This does not mean merely that his spirit, his soul, would soon pass out owing to death; because the spirit can become united with the beloved whilst yet in the body, a teaching well known to true brothers of the Rose-Cross. True brothers of the Rose-Cross know the place where Jesus went; they too can follow the path which Jesus trod. They seek the mystical marriage, the union between their soul and the beloved. 'You cannot follow me', Jesus said. No worldly-wise man can follow that path, only the truly humble, those who have seen God; the pure in heart, the single of purpose, the childlike, the simple, such as beloved Brother Francis of Assisi, only they can reach that place. The worldly-wise ever seek to kill the spiritual in man; that is the cause of conflict in the world today. The worldly-wise seek to kill the spirit.

Now let us turn to the gospel and see how these things are told.

(7 : 1–7) *After these things Jesus walked in Galilee: for he would not walk in Jewry, because the Jews sought to kill him. Now the Jews' feast of tabernacles was at hand. His brethren therefore said unto him, Depart hence, and go into Judaea, that thy disciples also may see the works that thou doest. For there is no man that doeth anything in secret, and he himself seeketh to be known openly. If thou do these things, shew thyself to the world. For neither did his brethren believe in him. Then Jesus said unto them, My time is not yet come: but your time is alway ready. The world cannot hate you; but me it hateth, because I testify of it, that the works thereof are evil.*

You see the conflict? The disciples were at that time in the world – of the world, worldly – they had not yet received illumination, they did not understand. But Jesus knew.

(7 : 8–9) *Go ye up unto this feast: I go not up yet unto this feast; for my time is not yet full come. When he had said these words unto them, he abode still in Galilee.*

The constant reference to *my time is not yet* we interpret to mean that the Master was waiting for the acceptable time of the Lord. He knew all things must come to pass in the fulness of time and that man cannot hurry the plans of God. People are always so eager, so anxious to get things done, to accomplish something, but the Master in his wisdom says, 'Wait!' Jesus was patient, but he was ready; he was completely in the hands of his Father. He did not rush in, as men so often do, where angels fear to tread. He remained quiet, waiting upon God's time. *My time is not yet.* See the tranquillity of his nature here revealed.

(7 : 10–16) *But when his brethren were gone up, then went he also up unto the feast, not openly, but as it were in secret. Then the Jews sought him at the feast, and said, Where is he? And there was much murmuring among the people concerning him: for some said, He is a good man: others said, Nay; but he deceiveth the people. Howbeit no man spake openly of him for fear of the Jews. Now about the*

midst of the feast Jesus went up into the temple and taught. And the Jews marvelled, saying, How knoweth this man letters, having never learned? Jesus answered them, and said, My doctrine is not mine, but his that sent me.

When the time was ripe, Jesus appeared in his body to teach the people. Immediately the worldly-minded cried, 'Who is this man? He is unlettered, unknown' – not recognising that Jesus taught not of himself, but that the great light, the divine truth, the universal wisdom was voiced through his lips. He had so attuned himself to the universal that he could be used as a channel through which all truth, all knowledge, all wisdom, could flow. In a very minor degree, this can be seen today, in highly developed people who can be used as channels or media for a higher intelligence. But one who has attained mastership, becomes a channel for pure and absolute universal truth.

(7 : 17–19) *If any man will do his will, he shall know of the doctrine, whether it be of God, or whether I speak of myself. He that speaketh of himself seeketh his own glory: but he that seeketh his glory that sent him, the same is true, and no unrighteousness is in him. Did not Moses give you the law, and yet none of you keepeth the law? Why go ye about to kill me?*

Do you not see how beautifully this truth is expressed? He that speaketh of himself speaketh only about himself and for his own ends; but he who is the instrument of God thinks not of his own glory; knows he is nothing and that all that he accomplishes is due to the light of God, the divine truth. To God be all honour and glory now and for evermore.

(7 : 20–21) *The people answered and said, Thou hast a devil: who goeth about to kill thee? Jesus answered and said unto them, I have done one work, and ye all marvel.*

Because Jesus had discernment regarding spiritual truth and reality, the intellectualists said, 'Thou hast a devil'. Is not that same attitude familiar today? Are not those clearly showing spiritual discernment sometimes credited with being on the side of the devil, or evil?

(7:22–29) *Moses therefore gave unto you circumcision: (not be-cause it is of Moses, but of the fathers;) and ye on the sabbath day circumcise a man. If a man on the sabbath day receive circumcision, that the law of Moses should not be broken; are ye angry at me, because I have made a man every whit whole on the sabbath day?*

Judge not according to the appearance, but judge righteous judgment.

Then said some of them of Jerusalem, Is not this he, whom they seek to kill? But, lo, he speaketh boldly, and they say nothing unto him. Do the rulers know indeed that this is the very Christ? Howbeit we know this man whence he is: but when Christ cometh, no man knoweth whence he is.

Then cried Jesus in the temple as he taught, saying, Ye both know me, and ye know whence I am: and I am not come of myself, but he that sent me is true, whom ye know not. But I know him: for I am from him and he hath sent me.

Jesus was aware of his divine origin, the source from which he came and of the object of his journey. As a contrast we find that worldly-wise man is confused, ignorant of his origin and of his destiny. Jesus clearly points out the difference between those who know and those who do not know. The true man, who sees the vision and knows whither he goeth, judges life according to the laws of the spirit, and according to spiritual values.

True values take much discerning, my brethren. You will find at every turn of life, in all your dealings with your fellows, in your emotions, your thoughts, the judgments which leap so quickly to your lips, that two standards of value will ever con-front you – the worldly, the material valuation, and the truly spiri-tual. On the one hand harshness, unbrotherliness, unkindness; on the other a brotherly endeavour to do unto others as ye would be done unto, to put yourself in the place of anyone who suffers injustice and misunderstanding. For then your soul yearns to gain knowledge and wisdom as to how to answer such problems;

and how to deal justly, wisely and lovingly with all the situations which arise in life.

(7 : 30–39) *Then they sought to take him: but no man laid hands on him, because his hour was not yet come. And many of the people believed on him, and said, When Christ cometh, will he do more miracles than these which this man hath done? The Pharisees heard that the people murmured such things concerning him; and the Pharisees and the chief priests sent officers to take him.*

Then said Jesus unto them, Yet a little while am I with you, and then I go unto him that sent me. Ye shall seek me, and shall not find me; and where I am, thither ye cannot come. Then said the Jews among themselves, Whither will he go, that we shall not find him? will he go unto the dispersed among the Gentiles, and teach the Gentiles? What manner of saying is this that he said, Ye shall seek me, and shall not find me: and where I am, thither ye cannot come?

In the last day, that great day of the feast, Jesus stood and cried, saying, If any man thirst, let him come unto me, and drink. He that believeth on me, as the scripture hath said, out of his belly shall flow rivers of living water. (But this spake he of the Spirit, which they that believe on him should receive: for the Holy Ghost was not yet given; because that Jesus was not yet glorified.)

This reference to 'living waters' we think alludes to the rock which Moses struck, from which the water flowed. We think that a more correct translation would make this clearer. When struck, the living waters flow out of the rock which formerly seemed so hard and unyielding; but only when struck in the true manner. Jesus said, *If any man thirst, let him come unto me, and drink* (37). He is referring to that truth which is in the Christ spirit, and which is that water of life which all shall some day drink. For there comes a time when each man will languish and faint through spiritual thirst and cry, 'Why does God do this to me?'. Thus cries the soul yearning for a draught of the living water which alone can quench its thirst. Then the hand of God will strike the rock of the worldly heart, probably in the form of suffering, sorrow or disappointment. The soul does not realise or recognise what is happening, but once the soul drinks and its thirst is assuaged there comes understanding and peace; for it has seen the power of the living God, it has drunk of that which only flows when the soul is struck (quickened) by the hand of God.

(7 : 40–43) *Many of the people therefore, when they heard this saying, said, Of a truth this is the Prophet. Others said, This is the Christ. But some said, Shall Christ come out of Galilee? Hath not the scripture said, That Christ cometh of the seed of David, and out of the town of Bethlehem, where David was? So there was a division among the people because of him.*

Does not this represent the world of today, and particularly the viewpoint of a materialist who clings to his own standard of values? If a prophet or spiritual teacher fails to conform to that standard, then he is no good. The critic lacks enough vision or discernment to see the truth indwelling in a man. The ways of the spirit, my brethren, are ever the gentle ways . . . meek, humble, lowly; and when these are seen, you can be sure that you are touching truth. Arrogance, self-advertisement, the flourish and sounding of trumpets . . . beware! 'I come in the little things', saith the Lord, 'in gentle things'.

The Eighth Chapter

THE LAW OF MAN AND THE LAW OF GOD

IN THE eighth chapter of St John we shall often find the same truth stated and restated. Notice how clear was the mind of Jesus, how completely he comprehended the essence of things, and also how dismally the intellectual thinkers in many instances failed to grasp the Master's meaning. Throughout this chapter we shall see how Jesus adhered logically to truth while some of his hearers – even his disciples – were off the mark. Jesus speaks of the absolute truth, life and love which comes only from God. The people who heard him had little realisation either of truth or of God. The Christ spirit within man's soul has to grow to manhood, and as it does, he will know truth and will express truth in thought, word and act. When it is young it is as a child and man does not comprehend it, and does not comprehend truth. It waits within the darkness of man's ignorance, and the darkness does not comprehend it.

In this chapter you will see again the two aspects of life set forth, and you will recognise them in your own everyday life. Jesus has a clear and perfect revelation of God his Father, and to this he holds fast. His actions, his thoughts, his words all express this pure sweet divine love; he has no room for anything else, he does not condemn. Early in this chapter we shall read the story of the woman taken in adultery, and note how eager were her accusers to persuade the Lord to condemn the woman. 'We caught her, we took her in sin. Now what have you to say?' they demanded, knowing that according to the law of Moses the woman merited stoning. Our interpretation is that the law of Moses is the earthly law, the law of the material world. But the laws of the world are not necessarily the laws of God; that is to say, they do not conform to the absolute truth of life. On the contrary, they often break the law of God. Do not misunderstand us: we do not suggest that you should disobey man-made law. Jesus said elsewhere: *Render to Caesar the things that are Caesar's, and to God the things that are God's* (Mk. 12 : 17). In man's present state of evolution and spiritual education there are many who can comprehend no other law but that of Moses. The people create for themselves their own laws; and according to a standard set by themselves they are governed. What we are trying to make clear is that two aspects, two laws exist – the law of God and the law of Moses.

The Jews hoped that they were going to trap the Master. 'What are you going to say to this woman?' they challenged. He did not look at them. He did not even look at the woman. He was concerned with writing something on the ground. See in this the gentle compassionate spirit of the Christ. He was ever thus. He did not look at the woman's accusers, for he did not want to accuse them even with a look, so he bent his head and wrote. In this simple act is a great depth of meaning. Jesus resorted to the law of God. He neither condemned the condemners nor the condemned, but endeavoured to set in motion by his very attitude certain spiritual forces which would *awaken conscience* in both accusers and accused. Is not that a wonderful attitude of mind? How many on earth can do that? And yet this is the very thing which happens in the spiritual world and in the outworking of the law of karma.

God has planted in the soul truth which, when stimulated through what you call conscience, can reveal the soul's errors to itself. No-one need hasten to condemn or set about righting any wrong by acting in accordance with the law of Moses. We are speaking now of trivial injustices which happen to us all. We can remain calm about these things, my friends. There is no need for self-justification if you endeavour to follow the law of God. This beautiful and wonderful truth, this law, works with absolute precision and exactitude. A soul is its own accuser. Once it sees itself – its lower self – revealed it will accuse itself and needs no outside judgment. Later in the chapter Jesus refers to a self or life which is 'beneath' (23). As the soul grows it will recognise that lower self which lies 'beneath', and will know when it has done wrong. Then a great love wells up in the soul. In the life beyond, once the conscience is awakened remorse will follow. Once true sadness and regret are felt the guide or teacher gently embraces the sinner, his pupil, never blaming, never harping upon what is past but gently leading the soul onward into some brighter region. For the soul then needs no more hell; it has had sufficient. True remorse can be so deep and so poignant that the soul needs no further judgment, only the healing balm of love.

This is what Jesus was endeavouring to teach by his actions. He did not condemn even the accusers. He did not wish to make them feel uncomfortable or guilty. They had yet to learn that he was expressing the spirit of his God in every thought and action. Jesus knew that God places man's judge within his own heart; man's judge is the God in man. *Hath no man condemned thee? She said, No man, Lord. And Jesus said unto her, Neither do I condemn thee: go, and sin no more* (10–11), although he knew that the woman had sinned. This means that while we must be able to recognise right from wrong, we may not pronounce judgment on the sinner because we cannot know his karma, nor the circumstances which have caused him to act in such a way. We dare not judge; and the older a soul grows the stronger grows its conviction of this truth.*

If only you could see the life of Jesus as we see it! Then you would see revealed the gentle, loving and true Son of God. The true teacher, the true son, withholds condemnation because he knows that in every man dwells a conscience, and he will help to awaken that conscience, help the soul to see itself. *Neither do I condemn thee: go, and sin no more.* Jesus' gentle words would go to the heart of the woman, and her heart, the voice of conscience, would speak to her.

Jesus proceeded to tell his hearers about the law of God. They tried to accuse him because he said that he spoke not of himself but of the Father. They charged him with having a demon because he claimed to be of God. Some people erroneously believe

* See Appendix, p. 187, 'Judgment'.

and claim they are inspired by great personalities in order to impress, in order to give weight to what they have to say. A true spiritual teacher has no need for this. A truly great man – either incarnate or discarnate – will not wish to draw attention to his own personality, for he knows that of himself he is nothing and that all that is good in him comes from God. Jesus denied that he had a demon. *I seek not mine own glory. . . . If I honour myself, my honour is nothing: it is my Father that honoureth me* (50, 54). He said, in so many words, 'All that I do is of the Father, God doeth the works – I am nothing. Had I a demon, I should not be giving all to God'.

Notice all through this chapter how this same gentle spirit shines with truth and love. Jesus speaks of those who sin as being 'dead', dead to the spiritual life, for it is the God expressed through man that gives him life. They could not be alive because life can only come to the Godlike man. The living soul is trying to express eternal life, or in the words of Jesus, not to do his own will, but the will of the Father. Such as these possess eternal life because it is indeed life to be expressing God, to be living God. To hate, to be cruel, to judge, to be governed by selfish desire, is death. The lower self spells death; the God in man is eternal life. Your bible tells you that at the last trump the dead shall rise from their graves. The 'dead' here are those enslaved by materialism; the sound of the trumpet is that mighty vibration which sweeps the soul and quickens the dead in spirit; they rise from the grave of materialism. This spiritual sound (the trumpet), this spiritual vibration quickens their souls when they are ready and they rise from the grave and go forth to meet the King, Christ, who said: *I, if I be lifted up . . . will draw all men unto me.*

Now you will see the thoughts that we have humbly presented for your consideration set forth much more clearly and beautifully.

(8 : 1–19) *Jesus went unto the mount of Olives. And early in the morning he came again into the temple, and all the people came unto him; and he sat down and taught them. And the scribes and Pharisees*

brought unto him a woman taken in adultery; and when they had set her in the midst, They say unto him, Master, this woman was taken in adultery, in the very act. Now Moses in the law commanded us, that such should be stoned: but what sayest thou? This they said, tempting him, that they might have to accuse him.

But Jesus stooped down, and with his finger wrote on the ground, as though he heard them not. So when they continued asking him, he lifted up himself, and said unto them, He that is without sin among you, let him first cast a stone at her. And again he stooped down, and wrote on the ground.

And they which heard it, being convicted by their own conscience, went out one by one, beginning at the eldest, even unto the last: and Jesus was left alone, and the woman standing in the midst.

When Jesus had lifted up himself, and saw none but the woman, he said unto her, Woman, where are those thine accusers? hath no man condemned thee? She said, No man, Lord. And Jesus said unto her, Neither do I condemn thee: go, and sin no more.

Then spake Jesus again unto them, saying, I am the light of the world: he that followeth me shall not walk in darkness, but shall have the light of life. The Pharisees therefore said unto him, Thou bearest record of thyself: thy record is not true. Jesus answered and said unto them, Though I bear record of myself, yet my record is true: for I know whence I came, and whither I go; but ye cannot tell whence I come, and whither I go. Ye judge after the flesh; I judge no man. And yet if I judge, my judgment is true: for I am not alone, but I and the Father that sent me. It is also written in your law, that the testimony of two men is true. I am one that bear witness of myself, and the Father that sent me beareth witness of me.

Then said they unto him, Where is thy Father?

Jesus answered, Ye neither know me, nor my Father: if ye had known me, ye should have known my Father also.

You see how plainly it is stated – *If ye had known me, ye should have known my Father*, meaning that if these men had been aware of the true life, if they had lived by love, they would instantly have recognised truth in the Master. If a man has once seen the true light he immediately recognises the light in his brother man. This is the true sign and grip of the Mason. It takes a God to see a God. *When ye have lifted up the Son of man, then shall ye know that I am he* (28) . . . Once a man has seen the true light, he will recognise the light in his brother.

(8 : 20–22) *These words spake Jesus in the treasury, as he taught in the temple: and no man laid hands on him; for his hour was not yet come. Then said Jesus again unto them, I go my way, and ye shall seek me, and shall die in your sins: whither I go, ye cannot come. Then said the Jews, Will he kill himself? because he saith, Whither I go, ye cannot come.*

You see, all the time their minds were set on the physical body, on the outer life. They did not grasp that Jesus was speaking of the spiritual life. *Whither I go ye cannot come.* They did not understand that he meant he was ascending to the heavens and that while they, because of sin, were lying in the grave, they could not go to the Father.

(8 : 23–26) *And he said unto them, Ye are from beneath; I am from above: ye are of this world; I am not of this world. I said therefore unto you, that ye shall die in your sins: for if ye believe not that I am he, ye shall die in your sins. Then said they unto him, Who art thou? And Jesus saith unto them, Even the same that I said unto you from the beginning. I have many things to say and to judge of you: but he that sent me is true; and I speak to the world those things which I have heard of him.*

Let us notice that word 'of'. *I have many things to say and to judge of you* – 'to judge *of* you', not 'to judge *you*'. We interpret this to mean that Jesus was able to judge between life and death, he was able to judge their degree of spiritual life or material deadness. In other words, they were his teachers, for what they did gave Jesus an increased understanding. You may look upon a certain act; you need not judge that act but you can learn from your observation of it to see more truly. You learn discrimination.

(8 : 27–59) *They understood not that he spake to them of the Father. Then said Jesus unto them, When ye have lifted up the Son of man, then shall ye know that I am he, and that I do nothing of myself; but as my Father hath taught me, I speak these things. And he that sent me is with me: the Father hath not left me alone; for I do always those things that please him. As he spake these words, many believed on him. Then said Jesus to those Jews which believed on him, If ye continue in my word, then are ye my disciples indeed; And ye shall know the truth, and the truth shall make you free.*

They answered him, We be Abraham's seed, and were never in bondage to any man: how sayest thou, Ye shall be made free?

Jesus answered them, Verily, verily, I say unto you, Whosoever committeth sin is the servant of sin. And the servant abideth not in the house for ever: but the Son abideth ever. If the Son therefore shall make you free, ye shall be free indeed. I know that ye are Abraham's seed: but ye seek to kill me, because my word hath no place in you. I speak that which I have seen with my Father: and ye do that which ye have seen with your father.

They answered and said unto him, Abraham is our father. Jesus saith unto them, If ye were Abraham's children, ye would do the works of Abraham. But now ye seek to kill me, a man that hath told you the truth, which I have heard of God: this did not Abraham. Ye do the deeds of your father.

Then said they to him, We be not born of fornication; we have one Father, even God.

Jesus said unto them, If God were your Father, ye would love me: for I proceeded forth and came from God; neither came I of myself, but he sent me. Why do ye not understand my speech? Even because ye cannot hear my word. Ye are of your father the devil, and the lusts of your father ye will do. He was a murderer from the beginning, and abode not in the truth, because there is no truth in him. When he speaketh a lie, he speaketh of his own: for he is a liar, and the father of it. And because I tell you the truth, ye believe me not. Which of you convinceth me of sin? And if I say the truth, why do ye not believe me? He that is of God heareth God's words; ye therefore hear them not, because ye are not of God.

Then answered the Jews, and said unto him, Say we not well that thou art a Samaritan, and hast a devil?

Jesus answered, I have not a devil; but I honour my Father, and ye do dishonour me. And I seek not mine own glory: there is one that seeketh and judgeth. Verily, verily, I say unto you, If a man keep my saying, he shall never see death.

Then said the Jews unto him, Now we know that thou hast a devil. Abraham is dead and the prophets; and thou sayest, If a man keep my saying, he shall never taste of death. Art thou greater than our father Abraham, which is dead? and the prophets are dead; whom makest thou thyself?

Jesus answered, If I honour myself, my honour is nothing: it is my Father that honoureth me; of whom ye say, that he is your God: Yet ye have not known him; but I know him: and if I should say, I know him not, I shall be a liar like unto you: but I know him, and keep his saying. Your father Abraham rejoiced to see my day: and he saw it, and was glad.

Then said the Jews unto him, Thou art not yet fifty years old, and hast thou seen Abraham?

Jesus said unto them, Verily, verily, I say unto you, Before Abraham was, I am.

Then took they up stones to cast at him: but Jesus hid himself, and went out of the temple, going through the midst of them, and so passed by.

We see throughout the reading two distinct lines of thought: we see Jesus speaking always from the spiritual aspect, from the eternal truth of God within him; and, on the other hand we see the Jews taking the earthly point of view. When Jesus spoke of their father they thought he referred to Abraham; but really he was speaking of spiritual things, and the 'father' here is the father of darkness, or of the lower self, all the lower aspects of humanity, or what orthodox people would term 'Satan'. (The word Satan does not mean to us quite what it does to the orthodox. Satan or Saturn represents the spirit of Lucifer, father of the spirits of wisdom which have a special concern with the evolution of mankind.) Jesus was referring to the lord of the negative or destructive aspect of life. Then comes that wonderful sentence *Before Abraham was, I am*, meaning that before Abraham lived among men that which was speaking in the Master was already in being. Long before the earth was created – before 'Abraham' – the Great Spirit (we call him Christ) was Son of God. Jesus said, *I am the way, the truth and the life* (14 : 6). But it was not Jesus the man who was speaking, it was the Christ, the third aspect of the Trinity saying 'I AM . . . I AM the truth within you . . . I AM the love within you . . . I AM the life within you for I AM come to give you eternal life'.

Then Jesus says *Your father Abraham rejoiced to see my day: and he saw it, and was glad*, suggesting, we think, that in all probability Abraham, the Jewish sage, entered into incarnation again about the same period as Jesus. He might even have been Zacharias or one of the disciples. At all events Jesus infers that he who was once Abraham, now reincarnated, was aware of and rejoicing in the works of Jesus at that very moment! Then the chapter ends as do other chapters with the words, *Jesus hid himself* (59) from the crowd. They took up stones – perhaps those same stones with which they were going to stone the woman, but he had made himself invisible. We know well that the sages in the Himalayas and in the Andes are able to appear and disappear at will when it serves their purpose. This is because the Masters understand how to quicken the vibration of the atoms of the body beyond the range of human eyesight. This is what Jesus did – made himself invisible to them, and disappeared from their midst.

The Ninth Chapter

THE MEANING OF SUFFERING

OUR THEME now concerns the soul or psyche more than the spirit, for the ninth chapter dwells largely upon reincarnation and karma. Some problems which come both to spiritual healers and their patients will probably be answered, because it is interesting to learn how psychic or soul unfoldment is reflected in the well-being or otherwise of the body.

Few people realise that their bodily life with its material and physical problems is the outermost expression of their inner life. By material problems we mean those pertaining to the material life – surroundings, work, and the financial perplexities which seem so important to the average Westerner. By physical problems we mean those which concern health of the body, and these arise from the soul. Now the problems of the soul, that is to say, difficulties which arise from psychological causes or from development of soul or psychic powers, find expression at last through the outer self, the material and physical life. So it is fairly safe to say that what man suffers on the physical plane sometimes results from soul-awakening or soul-quickening in some degree.

When reading the chapter bear this thought in mind, because it is the key to the Master's inner meaning. It is indeed a pity that so few understand the wonderful wisdom of Jesus. If you will give his words all your attention, you may find spiritual attunement and healing.

(9 : 1–41) *And as Jesus passed by, he saw a man which was blind from his birth. And his disciples asked him, saying, Master, who did sin, this man, or his parents, that he was born blind?*

Jesus answered, Neither hath this man sinned, nor his parents: but that the works of God should be made manifest in him. I must work the works of him that sent me, while it is day: the night cometh, when no man can work. As long as I am in the world, I am the light of the world.

When he had thus spoken, he spat on the ground, and made clay of the spittle, and he anointed the eyes of the blind man with the clay, and said unto him, Go, wash in the pool of Siloam (which is by interpretation, Sent.)

He went his way therefore, and washed, and came seeing. The neighbours therefore, and they which before had seen him that he was blind, said, Is not this he that sat and begged? Some said, This is he: others said, He is like him: but he said, I am he. Therefore said they unto him, How were thine eyes opened?

He answered and said, A man that is called Jesus made clay, and anointed mine eyes, and said unto me, Go to the pool of Siloam, and wash: and I went and washed, and I received sight.

Then said they unto him, Where is he?

He said, I know not.

They brought to the Pharisees him that aforetime was blind. And it was the sabbath day when Jesus made the clay, and opened his eyes. Then again the Pharisees also asked him how he had received his sight. He said unto them, He put clay upon mine eyes, and I washed, and do see.

Therefore said some of the Pharisees, This man is not of God, because he keepeth not the sabbath day. Others said, How can a man that is a sinner do such miracles? And there was a division among them. They say unto the blind man again, What sayest thou of him, that he hath opened thine eyes?

He said, He is a prophet.

But the Jews did not believe concerning him, that he had been blind, and received his sight, until they called the parents of him that had received his sight. And they asked them saying, Is this your son, who ye say was born blind? how then doth he now see? His parents answered them and said, We know that this is our son, and that he was born blind: But by what means he now seeth, we know not; or who hath opened his eyes, we know not: he is of age; ask him: he shall speak for himself.

75

These words spake his parents, because they feared the Jews: for the Jews had agreed already, that if any man did confess that he was Christ, he should be put out of the synagogue. Therefore said his parents, He is of age; ask him.

Then again called they the man that was blind, and said unto him, Give God the praise: we know that this man is a sinner.

He answered and said, Whether he be a sinner or no, I know not: one thing I know, that, whereas I was blind, now I see.

Then said they to him again, What did he to thee? how opened he thine eyes?

He answered them, I have told you already, and ye did not hear: wherefore would ye hear it again? will ye also be his disciples?

Then they reviled him, and said, Thou art his disciple; but we are Moses' disciples. We know that God spake unto Moses: as for this fellow, we know not from whence he is.

The man answered and said unto them, Why herein is a marvellous thing, that ye know not from whence he is, and yet he hath opened mine eyes. Now we know that God heareth not sinners: but if any man be a worshipper of God, and doeth his will, him he heareth. Since the world began was it not heard that any man opened the eyes of one that was born blind. If this man were not of God, he could do nothing.

They answered and said unto him, Thou wast altogether born in sins, and dost thou teach us? And they cast him out.

Jesus heard that they had cast him out; and when he had found him, he said unto him, Dost thou believe on the Son of God?

He answered and said, Who is he, Lord, that I might believe on him?

And Jesus said unto him, Thou hast both seen him, and it is he that talketh with thee.

And he said, Lord, I believe, And he worshipped him.

And Jesus said, For judgment I am come into this world, that they which see not might see; and that they which see might be made blind.

And some of the Pharisees which were with him heard these words, and said unto him, Are we blind also?

76

Jesus said unto them, If ye were blind, ye should have no sin: but now ye say, We see; therefore your sin remaineth.

This chapter deals not only with the physically blind, but with the soul-blind. It infers that the physically blind may have been blinded by a spiritual light which has awakened their psyche or their soul, which stirring caused in its turn physical blindness. The physically blind are not necessarily spiritually blind, indeed frequently we see the reverse is the case. For instance, Paul became sightless for the time being when the light of heaven fell upon him; although his soul was then awakened and quickened the heavenly light proved too much for his body at the time. This is what Jesus inferred when he touched the blind man with clay (yet another symbol of physical life). Laying clay upon the sightless eyes, he said that neither the man nor his parents had sinned. He was born blind in order that the law of God should be shown forth, demonstrating to those around that the divine law works unseen behind all life to bring about growth of the soul. We suggest that those who suffer – particularly because of blindness or defective vision – may have come to the last step upon a road of soul-cleansing or development. We are too apt to say, 'so and so is suffering as the result of karma'. This term is used a little loosely. Perhaps it would be more correct to say, 'so and so's body is suffering because he, the soul has reached the end of a certain path of growth or learning which has been undertaken'.

The body marks the limit, the end of a term of soul-experience; so we suggest that those who enjoy good health have in all probability completed a certain cycle or period of life which they had to traverse. You will say, 'But what about people who appear harsh and cruel to their fellows, and yet seem healthy and happy? Why is there so much suffering in the world? Why should innocent people be made to suffer?' Our reply is: There is no such thing as innocent suffering. Because the on-looker is unable to see far enough back, or far enough forward along the road of the sufferer, he remains ignorant of the spiritual law at work behind the suffering. The case of a person continuing to enjoy health and serenity throughout his incarnation, in spite of apparent shortcomings, is more difficult. We suggest the answer may be found in Jesus' words concerning the man who was born blind. The apparently healthy or carefree person is in all probability not working through the particular karma of a sick body in this incarnation. He may be learning his lessons, gaining valuable experience in a different way. Nevertheless his present life may be creating fresh karma, and he will be bound to meet in lives to come the result of seeds of selfishness, greed or carelessness sown today. That karma may show itself either in material or emotional suffering or, last of all, it will come out in physical suffering. When apparently incurable disease occurs, it means that a particular soul's weakness is being eliminated through that final physical climax of experience.

So, getting behind the Master's words in this ninth chapter, we begin to see an expanse of light. We suggest to you that psychic development (we do not mean merely the development of clairvoyance, clairaudience, trance mediumship, we mean the development of soul qualities) is of the utmost importance. Man should understand his potentialities, and also what may have happened in the past to cause him mental ill-health, sorrow, pain and the soul-development that is taking place in him as a result of that suffering. We do not like you to think of your troubles, accidents and tragedies as being visited upon you by a cruel God, but as part of the natural process of soul development. What appears to you to be disaster on the outer plane you will in the end recognise as all part of a wonderful pattern of your soul's growth towards happiness, light; and, if you like to use the word, salvation. A beautiful power is at work all the time, bringing the soul gradually to the fulness of spiritual life.

It is in this way that the Christ, the light, the life and truth in him is working through the soul of man and bringing him salvation. This is what is meant by salvation through Christ, a term to which many people object, saying that man is responsible for himself, and that as he sows, so shall he reap; that he cannot be saved by any other man. No, but he can save himself by living by the eternal spirit of Christ within himself. Christ is therefore the salvation of all mankind.

Try to be patient when you suffer. Try to accept the experiences of your life without resentment, my brethren, for resentment will only prolong the outworking of your karma. If you will accept all that happens to you as an outworking of a divine law which is all love, then you will rapidly pass through the lower planes of consciousness of earth's suffering, into light and happiness. Your heart will then sing the praises of your Creator, because you will know that even in your limited physical and material life, God is working out a beautiful purpose, bringing joyous flowers into bloom – the souls of men and women made perfect. You will now say, 'Are we, then, to accept all the sordid, evil conditions and cruelty that we see? Are we just to sit down and say, this is God's will! and ourselves do nothing to alleviate suffering?' My brethren, in some cases you are helpless to do anything; but you can and must help humanity by developing something of the love and compassion which the Master so clearly expressed. Go about your daily life full of sympathy and never turn away from suffering. Do all that you can to alleviate suffering at every level, for this is your opportunity to serve; above all give forth light and compassion, but always remember that, deeper than you can see, God is applying His own healing balm.

This is particularly applicable to the world of today. You see only one side of the picture revealed, but we come to show you the other side, to strengthen your faith and confidence in this infinite power, this divine love, which is working to bring good out of evil and bringing man to heaven out of his suffering. You fall into the same error today as did the Jews two thousand years ago. The Jews could see only the immediate outer conditions and happenings and were blind to the truths of the spirit; they even condemned the Master for healing on the Sabbath, being confined by the narrow conventions and customs of their religion and their country. They showed no understanding, no inner perception. Even the man who was healed was deemed a sinner by the Jews, and was rejected and reviled: and yet his having been born blind indicated to the Master that the man had come to the end of a certain lesson which his soul must learn. Now he was become psychically awake, psychically aware, for he had recognised the supreme light and life and truth of God in Jesus. This in itself would indicate to Jesus that the blind man had reached the end of some train of events or karma, which he had himself set up in the long past.*

Jesus inferred that the Jews were psychically blind albeit whole in body. This spiritual diagnosis by the Master should make us all think deeply. We look out upon mankind with hasty trivial judgments, criticisms, and condemnation of what we call shortcomings or sins, not always understanding the law at work behind human defects, bodily or mental. We impress upon you that the flooding in of the divine light, the life, the love, the truth of Christ will quickly throw out of the body remaining traces of past error. Such a purification can be accomplished in one incarnation and the soul enjoy freedom thereafter. Jesus demonstrated this fact by healing the man who was blind.

It is thought by some that all suffering is the result of a former sin. But Jesus, when asked who had sinned, the blind man he had healed, or his parents, said 'Neither'. It is true that the law of cause and effect is at work throughout human life, but there are instances in human life where suffering is not necessarily the direct result of mistakes in the past.

A soul returning to earth is given an opportunity of service to God and may accept affliction or suffering in order to demonstrate a lesson to humanity. Long before the soul descends through the spheres to be born into the body of flesh, an inner

---

* White Eagle has also pointed out in his teaching that sometimes physical suffering is accepted by the soul as an opportunity to help others to learn, and to serve. One thinks, for instance, of the parents of a child born with some severe handicap, and indeed often the love that the child brings, and the blessing that the parents experience as the result of their own selflessness, is a very rich and priceless gift, and the means of soul growth and expiation of karma.

voice, the voice of God, speaks to it offering it the opportunity of service and sacrifice. The man healed of blindness by the Master Jesus had volunteered, knew, long before he was born, that he would be used to demonstrate God's power working through the Master Jesus. He was willing to suffer, in order that others should be helped through his suffering. In his earthly consciousness he was not aware of this, any more than you are aware of inner truths in your outer mind, which is absorbed by the affairs of the world. You have neither the time nor the quiet to hear the voice of God speaking to you.

This explanation should enable you to view mankind with a greater love, for no one of us can judge another. We dare not judge. When you, my brother, have heard the inner voice, have heard the sound within the silence, you will have touched the mind of God, and you will know no separation from your brother man, no separation from your Father, for your Father in heaven is within the temple of your own being. And knowing the God within, you must love every man, for God is within him.

And so, we say to those who suffer – remember, it is not always a question of the working out of karma only. But in the deeper sense it is a way of service, for through suffering and the example of a noble life, others may learn and be helped. Always karma can be transmuted through the redeeming power of God's love working in man. We cannot too strongly emphasise the redeeming power of love.

I must work the works of him that sent me, while it is day: the night cometh, when no man can work. As long as I am in the world, I am the light of the world (4–5). So long as the I AM, the divine spark, the Son of God dwells in the flesh on the outermost plane of existence, for so long the I AM is the light of the world. But when the I AM withdraws itself from the world, then indeed the world is in darkness. This again has profound truth, and we are not sure that we can go as deeply into it as we would like at this stage. We suggest however that Jesus meant the 'night when no man can work' as a period upon which the soul enters, which is not death but rather passivity. Some say that it means a period between incarnations and indicates that when the soul leaves the body it will slumber until the next putting-forth of the soul. We do not subscribe to this view although we would not lay down hard and fast rules for there are degrees of unfoldment, and many levels of understanding.

Some souls, when they pass out of the body, do not immediately become conscious in the beyond, but may enter a period of passivity and remain in that condition for some time; they then awaken and possibly reincarnate without having experienced a great deal of conscious life while out of the body. This is not at all usual, however, least of all with more advanced souls. There is another interpretation – the space between the great life-cycles or ages, when there comes a period of passivity and rest, the 'night' in which no man works. This cosmic truth is hinted at in the book of Genesis. God created for six days; for six days He put forth energy, on the seventh, the day of cosmic rest, He rested. Jesus indicated that there is a period of time in the life of man, in the life of the world, which is as night, during which no man worked. It was a period of rest, of passivity, of sleep.

I must work the works of him that sent me, while it is day (4) means that when consciousness comes to man of the I AM while he dwells in the world, he must be active in putting forth the works of God. He cannot waste time. He must be continually expressing, living and evolving in the God-way and through the God-consciousness.

The Tenth Chapter

THE POWER OF LOVE

EVERY soul at some time must make its stand for truth, must stand forth as a warrior, and fight for what it knows to be right and true. Sometimes you may have described to you, or see in your meditations, a knight in shining armour, holding aloft the sword of truth. This shining knight symbolises your higher self, or your guide. This guide of your soul may come to you clothed in many different ways. He or she may adopt the astral body of any one of his or her previous incarnations or may wear the garment of pure spirit – shall we call it the heavenly raiment of flashing light and beauty? If you will visualise your guide in this way, you will attune yourself to the planes of pure spirit, and to do this must be your object each day if you would tread the way of the disciple.

It is a common error in early stages on the spiritual path to daydream, to live in a remote and nebulous state, sometimes of self-glorification, sometimes of an unbalanced emotionalism like that of a young pupil for an adored teacher. But the disciple on the path cannot live in this nebulous, dreamy state; he must come to grips with the problems of everyday life and human relationships in a practical and loving way, for the very best school for the pupil–disciple is that of everyday contacts with ordinary people in an everyday world. The friction of daily life is the process which smoothes off the surfaces of the 'rough ashlar' of the apprentice so that it becomes the perfect cube of the master Mason.

No man can run away from his life-experience. We say this with great earnestness. However often you run away from your lessons, again and again and again will you be faced with the same cycle of experience until some weakness or defect is at last erased, some lesson learned.

THE LIVING WORD OF ST JOHN

God, the supreme light and glory of life, is all-wise, and His nature is love; all creation is subject to the law of love. Therefore we should welcome those very circumstances against which our lower nature and our lower self rebels, and be brave warriors in the field of battle, knowing that the end is love. The Bhagavad Gita, one of the great scriptures of the world, tells the same story of the conflict between man's higher and his lower self, the former knowing inwardly, intuitively, the way of love, the latter eager for ease, comfort and self-glory.

This tenth chapter of St John which we shall review now presents yet another of the keys to spiritual life. It deals primarily with the power of love. How few of those enslaved by the body can glimpse the wonder, the sweetness and divine purity of love! Of course there are many degrees of love; but the truth of love is the keystone or cornerstone in the building of your own temple and of the great temple of the universe. The object of all spiritual striving, the answer to all problems, fears and pain, the strong victor over death – is love.

All this you will find woven into this tenth chapter of St John's gospel.

We learn our lessons in the primary school on earth. If we observe the human dramas enacted around us in life, and indeed search our own lives to find the cause of our suffering, we shall often find it to be either lack or misapplication of love; or else misunderstanding of love, or love without wisdom. There are many degrees, many different manifestations of the quality of love. The love which first manifests through the animal nature of man gradually becomes refined until at last it can be seen, pure and selfless, in the perfected soul of the initiate and master; in a love which enters into the life and soul of every man and woman, feeling with them, sharing their sorrows and their joy, a love which knows no separation and which is ever united with the Father Mother God. This teaching is contained in the principles which we gave for the guidance of our Lodge, expressed in the reunion of the child with the Father Mother God, the reunion of the holy family.

Those who remain isolated from their fellows, who stand aloof from what they call the lower aspect of life, may be further removed from the attainment of such an ideal of love than simpler men or women whose love seems mainly of the body; for the lessons of life can be learned in the primary class of human love – the love of man for his wife, or of brother for sister, mother for child, father for son, friend for friend. This emotion of human love is the beginning, and holds seed and promise of divine love. Without a spontaneous urge to love rather than to be loved there can be no opening of the bud. Most human beings long to be loved; some spontaneously give forth love because they cannot help themselves, because it has grown as natural to think of, to care for, and to cherish the beloved as to breathe and sleep.

This is one of the lessons which awaits the soul in the halls of learning beyond this physical life. As it becomes accustomed to its new state of life and begins to recognise the companionship of the guide and teacher by its side, gradually the thought awakens, 'I love . . . I love' rather than 'I want to be loved'. This urge to love comes from an expansion of consciousness, a recognition that love should permeate and irradiate every act, and thought and motive of human life, a love which is always outgoing, outpouring itself without thought and without restraint.

In this chapter the Master has this vision of love, feels this emotion, this great truth and light, when he speaks of the door leading to the fold, and of his sheep. There is a door into the fold and the sheep will follow the shepherd through it. That door is love. The shepherd can be some spiritual teacher who can inspire you with confidence, faith and love. The true shepherd enters through the door of love, and the sheep instinctively, intuitively recognise and follow after.

The Master referred to certain wolves seeking to devour the sheep. These are the false teachers, the false leaders, who try to dominate others by reason of intellectual attainment or occult power, or through – shall we say – spurious teachings they would inculcate.

All the masters throughout the ages, who have come at different stages on the path of the spiritual evolution of man, have come to bring the truth to man, and this truth is the same yesterday, today and for ever. Every master has taught in his own language and in his own way the one great truth, how man can find for himself the way into the spiritual worlds, the way into the centre.

Think of the vast circle of life, the Sun, then look to the centre, the inmost heart of the Sun – some of our brethren would describe it as the dot within the circle. This is your goal. And this is what every master endeavours to show his people – how to enter the spiritual worlds through that gateway.

Now Jesus spoke of himself as the shepherd, and he said more than once: *I am the good shepherd, and know my sheep* (14). Now, do not misunderstand this, my children. He does not mean to segregate certain people of a certain faith and call them his sheep. No! He is referring to the individual spirit in every man. Every man who responds to the spirit of love is going to find truth, is going to follow the good shepherd along the pathway, and through the gate into the fold – in other words, into cosmic consciousness, where all barriers dissolve, and the sheep instantly respond to the voice of the shepherd. Every soul who follows that one true way enters into the fold, or into cosmic consciousness, because that soul recognises that it is a part of the whole, is no longer separated from anything or any person. This means that he takes upon himself the sorrows and the joys of all mankind. Don't forget this, my children; when you enter into the fold, into the divine life and consciousness, you enter into all joy and knowledge. Life is no longer limited in any way. Life is one whole, it is infinity and eternity.

The Master, the good shepherd, knows his sheep, because he knows their heart, their vibration. Your thoughts, your prayers, your aspirations create a vibration, not only on the lower ethers but right through the spheres to the centre, to the very throne of God.

(10 : 1) *Verily, verily, I say unto you, He that entereth not by the door into the sheepfold, but climbeth up some other way, the same is a thief and a robber.*

The path into the fold is the path of love, of gentleness, self-discipline. The thieves and robbers are those who, refusing this path, try to enter the fold by some other means. There are those for instance who, eager for knowledge, try to force an entrance through mental or magical powers, through the power of intellect. It is one thing to read about spiritual truth, to know it with the mind, but quite another so to live as to express that truth in every thought and word and act. Jesus explains elsewhere that the true way is narrow, that the spiritual life is difficult, particularly at first. There are difficulties at every step, but gradually the soul grows stronger, steadier and more poised and able to withstand the storms. There is no short cut into heaven. You cannot climb in through any window; you have to enter through the door of self-discipline. So welcome each rebuff. Grasp your nettle, and accept every disappointment as an opportunity offered you to step forward on your path.

(10 : 2–3) *But he that entereth in by the door is the shepherd of the sheep. To him the porter openeth; and the sheep hear his voice: and he calleth his own sheep by name, and leadeth them out.*

We suggest that the 'porter', the keeper of the door, is man's inner consciousness, the Christ within, which recognises the true from the false and refuses to let anything pass that is not true, not real.

Everyone that has awakened to the meaning of love instantly recognises the voice of love in another, or in his teacher. This recognition is akin to the grip of the Freemason and the secret signs of the mystery schools. A soul who has passed through the initiation of love does not need to speak, for it radiates light and truth and all the master's sheep will respond.

(10 : 4–5) *And when he putteth forth his own sheep, he goeth before them, and the sheep follow him: for they know his voice. And*

a stranger will they not follow, but will flee from him: for they know not the voice of strangers.

Who are the strangers? Those who do not ring true. Those who do not speak with the voice of love. Those alien to love are strangers to those who love.

(10:6–10) *This parable spake Jesus unto them: but they understood not what things they were which he spake unto them. Then said Jesus unto them again, Verily, verily, I say unto you, I am the door of the sheep. All that ever came before me are thieves and robbers; but the sheep did not hear them. I am the door: by me if any man enter in, he shall be saved, and shall go in and out, and find pasture. The thief cometh not, but for to steal, and to kill, and to destroy: I am come that they might have life, and that they might have it more abundantly.*

We think Jesus is referring to the anti-Christ whose method is not the way of love, of gentleness, of truth.

Salvation comes to the soul only through love, through illumination of the heart centre. In the heart centre is the jewel, the Christ light. People may study comparative religion for years, may have an accumulation of knowledge intellectually; but we say again that there is only one way for the soul's salvation and redemption, and that is simply through the love of the Christ.

(10:11–13) *I am the good shepherd: the good shepherd giveth his life for the sheep. But he that is an hireling, and not the shepherd, whose own the sheep are not, seeth the wolf coming, and leaveth the sheep, and fleeth: and the wolf catcheth them, and scattereth the sheep. The hireling fleeth, because he is an hireling, and careth not for the sheep.*

He who *careth not for the sheep* is one who cannot stand the test of love.*

(10:14–15) *I am the good shepherd, and know my sheep, and am known of mine. As the Father knoweth me, even so know I the Father: and I lay down my life for the sheep.*

* See Appendix, p. 188, 'Mind'.

The soul initiated into the great realm of love surrenders all selfish desire. No longer does the 'I' rule; the 'I', the self, is surrendered; all thought for self is laid aside. The statement *I lay down my life for the sheep* means that such an initiate loves even the darkest sinner. This you cannot understand yet. It means that the initiate of love must go so far as to love and absorb into himself the sorrows and evil of earth and so change bad into good, darkness into light. At some time in every life will come the soul's surrender of everything, the laying down of self-life for the sake of the whole – a surrender again described in the Revelation of St John (4:10), in the casting down of the crowns of the elders before the throne of God. No soul can remain selfish and isolated and retain what it believes it possesses. It must give and give and give in love to all creation, every condition in life.

(10:16) *And other sheep I have, which are not of this fold: them also I must bring, and they shall hear my voice; and there shall be one fold, and one shepherd.*

We have already spoken of this. It does not refer to different races, different nationalities. It means that where the one true illumination shines through any teacher he is of the one fold. There are also others who are good, well meaning, and faithful, but who have not yet seen the flashing jewel of love. When they awake to the Cosmic Christ they too will be gathered in. Although there are many paths, all must eventually come into the one supreme light.

(10:17–18) *Therefore doth my Father love me, because I lay down my life, that I might take it again. No man taketh it from me, but I lay it down of myself. I have power to lay it down, and I have power to take it again. This commandment have I received of my Father.*

The 'laying down of life', we interpret as meaning the complete surrender of self to the Supreme, as we have already said. There is another interpretation, and this is that a great and ancient one can lay aside his body, it can be dissolved at will and for a purpose; and at some future time it can be taken up again, or resuscitated.

(10:19–24) *There was a division therefore again among the Jews for these sayings. And many of them said, He hath a devil, and is mad: why hear ye him? Others said, These are not the words of him that hath a devil. Can a devil open the eyes of the blind? And it was at Jerusalem the feast of the dedication, and it was winter. And Jesus walked in the temple in Solomon's porch. Then came the Jews round about him, and said unto him, How long dost thou make us to doubt? If thou be the Christ, tell us plainly.*

The Sage has no need to declare himself. The light and power which shine forth from him should be sufficient testimony. The sheep will recognise their shepherd, not by what he says, not even by what he knows, but by his emanation of sincerity, affection and purity.

You will notice that Jesus was said to be 'walking in Solomon's porch', when he said these words – in the porch of the Sun, of the great light. In other words, the truth he voiced came from the universal Sun, from the supreme light. You see the wonderful esoteric meaning of this statement?

(10:25–42) *Jesus answered them, I told you, and ye believed not: the works that I do in my Father's name, they bear witness of me. But ye believe not, because ye are not of my sheep, as I said unto you. My sheep hear my voice, and I know them, and they follow me: And I give unto them eternal life; and they shall never perish, neither shall any man pluck them out of my hand.*

My Father, which gave them me, is greater than all; and no man is able to pluck them out of my Father's hand. I and my Father are one. Then the Jews took up stones again to stone him. Jesus answered them, Many good works have I shewed you from my Father; for which of those works do ye stone me?

The Jews answered him, saying, For a good work we stone thee not; but for blasphemy; and because that thou, being a man, makest thyself God.

Jesus answered them, Is it not written in your law, I said, Ye are gods? If he called them gods, unto whom the word of God came, and the scripture cannot be broken; Say ye of him, whom the Father hath sanctified, and sent into the world, Thou blasphemest; because I said, I am the Son of God? If I do not the works of my Father, believe me not. But if I do, though ye believe not me, believe the works: that ye may know, and believe, that the Father is in me, and I in him.

Therefore they sought again to take him: but he escaped out of their hand. And went away again beyond Jordan into the place where John at first baptized; and there he abode. And many resorted unto him, and said, John did no miracle: but all things that John spake of this man were true. And many believed on him there.

When once the sheep recognises the shepherd, when once the soul has seen the true light, it can no longer be separated from the master, from love. We would like to share the profound truth that the initiated, those reborn through true love, can always be recognised by their fellows. When following your path try to reflect the true light of this Sun, this love, this beauty, in your life and in your heart. Endeavour to respond at all times to the impetus towards kindliness and selflessness. This is the true way. 'I love, I love . . . I am love. I come to help my companion, not to stone him.'

The silent forms of the invisible brethren radiate light; they give with such infinite tenderness! They speak deep in your heart and tell you that as you are true and faithful in little things, in simple daily tests, so you rise step by step into the heaven world. Would that we could describe the halls of light and wisdom that await you, my brother, and you, my sister, where you may enter and receive the supreme blessing of eternal happiness!

Let us stand together before the throne to pray that we may not fail in our work to help our brother man to see, to know, and to become one of the vast company of the blessed in heaven. Dear God, help us in this. Amen.

The Eleventh Chapter

THE RESURRECTION OF MAN

IN THE chapter we are about to study we shall find a wonderful spiritual and inner meaning in the words of the Master, not to be interpreted by the mind alone, but by the Christ spirit within, which alone reveals truth, and life and love.

(11:1–26) *Now a certain man was sick, named Lazarus, of Bethany, the town of Mary and her sister Martha. (It was that Mary which anointed the Lord with ointment, and wiped his feet with her hair, whose brother Lazarus was sick.) Therefore his sisters sent unto him, saying, Lord, behold, he whom thou lovest is sick. When Jesus heard that, he said, This sickness is not unto death, but for the glory of God, that the Son of God might be glorified thereby. Now Jesus loved Martha, and her sister, and Lazarus. When he had heard therefore that he was sick, he abode two days still in the same place where he was. Then after that saith he to his disciples, Let us go into Judaea again. His disciples say unto him, Master, the Jews of late sought to stone thee; and goest thou thither again?*

Jesus answered, Are there not twelve hours in the day? If any man walk in the day, he stumbleth not, because he seeth the light of this world. But if a man walk in the night, he stumbleth, because there is no light in him. These things said he: and after that he saith unto them, Our friend Lazarus sleepeth; but I go, that I may awake him out of sleep.

Then said his disciples, Lord, if he sleep, he shall do well. Howbeit Jesus spake of his death: but they thought that he had spoken of taking of rest in sleep.

Then said Jesus unto them plainly, Lazarus is dead. And I am glad for your sakes that I was not there, to the intent ye may believe; nevertheless let us go unto him.

Then said Thomas, which is called Didymus, unto his fellow disciples, Let us also go, that we may die with him.

Then when Jesus came, he found that he had lain in the grave four days already. Now Bethany was nigh unto Jerusalem, about fifteen furlongs off: And many of the Jews came to Martha and Mary, to comfort them concerning their brother. Then Martha, as soon as she heard that Jesus was coming, went and met him: but Mary sat still in the house. Then said Martha unto Jesus, Lord, if thou hadst been here, my brother had not died. But I know, that even now, whatsoever thou wilt ask of God, God will give it thee.

Jesus saith unto her, Thy brother shall rise again.

Martha saith unto him, I know that he shall rise again in the resurrection at the last day.

Jesus said unto her, I am the resurrection and the life: he that believeth in me, though he were dead, yet shall he live: And whosoever liveth and believeth in me shall never die. Believest thou this?

I am the resurrection and the life – meaning that the 'I AM' or the Christ spirit within the heart of man is the divine spark of light which is the resurrection and which is the life. The Christ spirit, the recreative power and life dwells within every one of God's children. I AM the love within you. I AM the life within you. I bring eternal life to you.

(10:27–29) *She saith unto him, Yea, Lord: I believe that thou art the Christ, the Son of God, which should come into the world. And when she had so said, she went her way, and called Mary her sister secretly, saying, The Master is come, and calleth for thee. As soon as she heard that, she arose quickly, and came unto him.*

We see in this, as in other chapters, two distinct lines of thought, two levels of understanding – the spiritual and the worldly. On the one hand, there is the Master, Jesus the Christ, who understood the inner meaning of life, who understood spiritual law, and we see him expressing the law of the spirit without wavering. On the other, we see how the Jews and the ordinary people – even those of the disciples whose eyes were not yet opened – spoke from the mind, from the material self, as befits men of the world. We see that Jesus abode always by the spiritual life and the spiritual law and interpreted everything that happened by the light of real truth, by the light of Christ within. This is something we all have to learn to do, for once men or women have seen the spiritual life and law revealed, they must afterwards apply spiritual law to every detail of life. There can be no exception, for as another wise one has said 'between right and wrong, there can be no compromise'. This is why many suffer when they set out upon the spiritual path. They are not strong enough to stand by their spiritual convictions; they continue to see their problems from the material aspect and to be influenced by material considerations instead of remaining firmly on the spiritual path. Again there can be no compromise. Once you have set your feet upon the spiritual path do not be dragged into the vortex of materiality or you will again become spiritually blinded. If you endeavour to see all your problems from a spiritual viewpoint, to see truth in life and in man's soul, then you will undoubtedly see the glory of God.

The death of Lazarus can and should be interpreted in this spiritual sense. Some schools of thought prefer to regard the story solely as a record of a physical miracle, and we are not suggesting that it was not; but the primary object of the story is to demonstrate the awakening of the spiritual life in Lazarus. Study the chapter and you will see what we mean, for you will find little stress laid upon the bodily death, which the Master did not seem to think important. He was, however, concerned with the raising of Lazarus from the spiritual death.

When Jesus proposed to visit the home of Lazarus, his disciples protested, *Master, the Jews of late sought to stone thee; and goest thou thither again? Jesus answered, Are there not twelve hours in the day?* (8–9), saying, in other words, there is a time for everything. My time to leave the physical body is planned. It does not matter; so long as my life is spent in service, God will protect me. This suggests that man must not be foolish enough to tempt Providence by needlessly laying himself open to danger, but should the service of God call, he can go where he will in perfect composure, certain that although there may be danger, his time will not come until that service is accomplished.

We make this clear; do not break spiritual law by being careless or reckless but, on the other hand, if you are about your Father's business and working in harmony with spiritual law, you will be protected whatever the danger. *Are there not twelve hours in the day?* Those who quietly obey the law have nothing to fear, for everything comes into the plan and there is a time and place for everything; and when all is said and done and a man's time is come, the finest attitude for facing death is this tranquil acceptance of the perfection and exactitude of God's plan.

Learn to live in accord with the spiritual law, with the law of God, of harmony and well-being. Do not violate the laws of God which operate within your own body, for your body is a temple of God, and not yours to take into danger, to overtire, to knock about and to deny natural and wholesome food. You are breaking the spiritual law by so doing. Your body must be bathed and kept clean; it must be fed wisely, treated with respect, it may not be overworked or over-indulged; so that when its time has come the soul will arise and go forth . . . 'I come, Lord; I have heard Thy call!'

So long as you obey the spiritual law you can live your days with perfect tranquillity. Obey the true call of the spirit even if you should encounter danger, for when you are about your Father's business, all is well. Whatever happens all is well.

If any man walk in the day – which means in the light – *he stumbleth not* (9). If you are working according to the laws of the spirit, it is daylight for you. This we have already explained. If darkness and confusion reign in the soul, the man stumbles.

Verse 41 tells of the rolling back of the stone from the grave. We interpret that stone to mean the stone of the worldly mind which seals a man within his grave. The material scientist, the material religionist, the material man in any department of life is as one in a closed box, in a grave, sealed in by a stone of mortal mind, of materiality. In other words the man, because he is dead

95

to spiritual things, has put himself into a grave, and then others of like mind roll the stone before him and seal him in. Is not the world always ready to roll the stone of materiality on to a man and seal him in his grave? And how difficult it is for the man to free himself!

Those who though living are thus dead can only be restored to life by the Word, by the trumpet call, by response of their innermost to Christ the Son, the true spiritual brother of the spiritually dead. Christ the Son called to Lazarus, through the Master, and he rose from the grave. Thus the spiritually dead can be recalled to life, but God needs a pure and perfect channel through which to recall the dead to life.

Throughout the gospel of St John, Christ speaks through the Master's lips and life. This same raising of Lazarus is continually going on in the world about us. We ourselves, like Lazarus, have probably lain in our grave until the Godlike in us has responded at last and we have arisen in answer to the call.

(11:30–44) *Now Jesus was not yet come into the town, but was in that place where Martha met him. The Jews then which were with her in the house, and comforted her, when they saw Mary, that she rose up hastily and went out, followed her, saying, She goeth unto the grave to weep there. Then when Mary was come where Jesus was, and saw him, she fell down at his feet, saying unto him, Lord, if thou hadst been here, my brother had not died.*

When Jesus therefore saw her weeping, and the Jews also weeping which came with her, he groaned in the spirit, and was troubled, And said, Where have ye laid him? They said unto him, Lord, come and see. Jesus wept. Then said the Jews, Behold how he loved him! And some of them said, Could not this man, which opened the eyes of the blind, have caused that even this man should not have died?

Jesus therefore again groaning in himself cometh to the grave. It was a cave, and a stone lay upon it. Jesus said, Take ye away the stone.

Martha, the sister of him that was dead, saith unto him, Lord, by this time he stinketh: for he hath been dead four days.

Jesus saith unto her, Said I not unto thee, that, if thou wouldest believe, thou shouldest see the glory of God? Then they took away the stone from the place where the dead was laid.

And Jesus lifted up his eyes and said, Father, I thank thee that thou hast heard me. And I knew that thou hearest me always; but because of the people which stand by I said it, that they may believe that thou hast sent me. And when he thus had spoken, he cried with a loud voice, Lazarus, come forth. And he that was dead came forth, bound hand and foot with grave-clothes: and his face was bound about with a napkin. Jesus saith unto them, Loose him, and let him go.

You notice that Jesus said to the mourners, *Loose him, and let him go*, rather indicating that worldly companions can help to bind a soul. Truly others have power to hold you down to a life of materialism. Their influence and thought can dominate you until at last you hear the voice. Then nothing can bind you, nothing hold you.

Notice that Martha said that the body of Lazarus might have become corrupt. Here again the Master, putting aside all else, speaks of the glory of God, refusing to recognise decay or death. He sees only the light of God illumining the soul of Lazarus.

Previous to this is a passage which refers to the weeping of Mary and Martha. Jesus too wept, and those looking on said, *Behold how he loved him!* (36), thinking that Jesus was weeping for the loss of his friend; but this was not the reason for Jesus' grief. He was weeping because he was sharing wholly the feelings of his friends – an example of true brotherhood. You will notice that Mary at first did not come out to meet the Master but remained quietly in meditation. Mary had already truly sensed who was the Christ working through Jesus. Martha, however, was busy with the household, and so full of the news of the death that she has to run and remonstrate with the Master. Mary remained still for she better understood the relationship between the Master, herself and the others. We should say that

Mary had been initiated into true brotherhood through what is sometimes called the feast or ceremony of love, when the spirit and soul of the initiated becomes merged with all its other brethren, which only happens when the soul is raised to consciousness and understanding of true love. To become truly initiated into the brotherhood of the Christ light means that the brother is so merged into the sorrows and joys of others that he feels with them; he not only looks upon suffering with sympathy, but he identifies himself with the sufferer. This is a state to which we have all to come. And when all humanity can thus become one in spirit, what a change will follow! There will be no more wanton or thoughtless cruelty, for a man will know that if he inflicts suffering on his brother, he himself suffers.

True brotherhood means a heart attuned to a brother's heart, the eyes wet with the tears the brother sheds. This is why Jesus weeps. He weeps because Mary is weeping. He feels the bitterness and sorrow she is experiencing through loss of her brother. He even groans in spirit when he goes forth to call Lazarus, because he too is imprisoned within the grave where Lazarus lies. His whole being enters into Lazarus and raises him from death to life.

Some power of imagination must awake before the true brother understands another's suffering. The development of imagination is a necessary part of man's awakening, but you will not attain this through trying mentally, but rather by the development of feeling, of awareness, through meditation and through experience. It is imagination which enables the seer to enter into the feelings of another, to become for the moment the spirit from which the message comes. The materialist and intellectualist lacks that spiritual awareness.

(11:45–57) *Then many of the Jews which came to Mary, and had seen the things which Jesus did, believed on him. But some of them went their ways to the Pharisees, and told them what things Jesus had done. Then gathered the chief priests and the Pharisees a council, and said, What do we? for this man doeth many miracles. If we let him thus alone, all men will believe on him: and the Romans shall come and take away both our place and nation. And one of them, named Caiaphas, being the high priest that same year, said unto them, Ye know nothing at all, Nor consider that it is expedient for us, that one man should die for the people, and that the whole nation perish not. And this spake he not of himself: but being high priest that year, he prophesied that Jesus should die for that nation; And not for that nation only, but that also he should gather together in one the children of God that were scattered abroad.*

Then from that day forth they took counsel together for to put him to death. Jesus therefore walked no more openly among the Jews; but went thence unto a country near to the wilderness, into a city called Ephraim, and there continued with his disciples. And the Jews' passover was nigh at hand: and many went out of the country up to Jerusalem before the passover, to purify themselves. Then sought they for Jesus, and spake among themselves, as they stood in the temple, What think ye, that he will not come to the feast? Now both the chief priests and the Pharisees had given a commandment, that, if any man knew where he were, he should shew it, that they might take him.

Even today the individual is being persecuted, allegedly for the sake of the community. Yet Jesus said that every soul was of account in the Father's eyes. *Are not two sparrows sold for a farthing? and one of them shall not fall on the ground without your Father. But the very hairs of your head are all numbered* (Mt. 10:29–30). The world says that the individual may be sacrificed if it is expedient, but the law of the spirit is that every soul is precious. What we read into these last few verses is that the world was out to slay Jesus, but that he would wait until the twelfth hour of the day when his time had come. Then he would be ready to give himself up as the gospel tells.

Thus two parallel lines of thought dominate this chapter. The usual interpretation is material, and concerns the raising of the physical body of Lazarus. But Jesus was ever working with the spiritual law, his supreme object being to bring light, life and truth to the soul of his brother man. To this end he lived, died and rose again.

The purpose of every man's life is the resurrection of man from the tomb of the lower mind, of physical matter; a breaking of the bonds of the tomb of earth and rising in understanding and mastery, so that all matter, all ether, all radiations of thought, may be penetrated by the spirit of love, of Christ, so that every form of life may be alive with the spirit of the Creator, of Christ.

This is the meaning of the resurrection and the regeneration of man and form by the true life of spirit.

The works that I do shall he do also. Every man will in due time become fully conscious of the eternal life and power and beauty of the Christ spirit in himself – and in his brother.

The Twelfth Chapter

THE PURIFICATION OF THE BODY

ONE CENTRAL truth is expressed throughout St John's gospel, a truth which encompasses the whole of man's being, that of spiritualising the whole of life and bringing it into perfect balance. We know some teachers advocate the killing of natural desires and the mortification of the flesh, regarding this as the only way to eternal life; but we do not agree with this. On the contrary we would see life on earth as something very beautiful, to be enjoyed and experienced to the full.

For instance, when you eat do not do so thoughtlessly but with enjoyment. See God's bounty in your food, and praise your creator for it, knowing that God has given you food for the purpose not only of feeding your body but nourishing the psyche or etheric body. See the best, see God in friends and happy family, receive them into your heart, accept them as gifts from God. Enjoy every faculty of the body, the soul and the spirit, and praise God every moment of your life. Praise Him for all nature, for the animals, for the arts and crafts and all that beautifies life.

We believe that human life should blossom into perfect form, perfect health, perfect radiance. Like a beautiful rose life should find sufficient nourishment for its roots, its stem, its leaves and its fruit in the gifts of the earth, and like a rose should take its place in the sunlight and glorify God. The body, being the temple of God, should be cared for, clothed as far as possible in immaculate clothing. It should have periods of harmonious re-creation, leisure for physical and mental development and interest, opportunities for spiritual culture. All the vehicles contained in the being of man – that is, the physical and etheric, the astral, the mental, and the celestial – should be evolving towards perfection and expressing the true life of God. As things are, alas, even the body is denied the conditions it needs, while the mental body is often overstimulated and unsuitably fed and the astral or desire body uncontrolled. This lack of control releases desires and passions which are eventually reflected as disease in the physical and mental body and so the whole being becomes out of harmony.

Jesus speaks of this in our present chapter, saying that man must lose his mortal life to gain the true life. We would stress the 47th verse: *I came not to judge the world, but to save the world.* What did the Master mean? We shall have to digress for a moment, to repeat that when the physical body dies what is known as the etheric body, sometimes called the etheric double, is withdrawn from the physical. We have already explained that this etheric body consists of two parts. That part which bears the seed of eternal life is built into the temple of the soul, and that part which is of the earth eventually disintegrates and dies.

Through aspiration of the soul, eternal life is given to the finer etheric body. This etheric body, or psyche, is created by man's life as a whole, his actions, aspirations and desires, and all that he expresses in everyday life. This is why it is so important to live in the material world and physical body with the object of manifesting God in every detail of life.

Thus when Jesus said, *I came not to judge the world, but to save the world* (47), he meant just what we are saying; that through the spirit of Christ, man's life is made harmonious and perfected. In this way Christ is saving man, raising him up to heaven. Did he not say, *And I, if I be lifted up from the earth, will draw all men unto me* (32)?

Now, let us read the words of the gospel:

(12:1–8) *Then Jesus six days before the passover came to Bethany, where Lazarus was which had been dead, whom he raised from the dead. There they made him a supper; and Martha served: but Lazarus was one of them that sat at the table with him. Then took Mary a pound of ointment of spikenard, very costly, and anointed the feet of Jesus, and wiped his feet with her hair: and the house was filled with the odour of the ointment. Then saith one of his disciples, Judas Iscariot, Simon's son, which should betray him, Why was not this ointment sold for three hundred pence, and given to the poor? This he said, not that he cared for the poor; but because he was a thief, and had the bag, and bare what was put therein. Then said Jesus, Let her alone: against the day of my burying hath she kept this. For the poor always ye have with you; but me ye have not always.*

Martha, you will remember, blamed Mary because she neglected to help in the domestic work. Jesus said, *Mary hath chosen that good part* (Lk. 10:42), meaning that Martha on that occasion should have recognised what was happening within Mary. Martha did not know, but Jesus was aware, that Mary was opening her innermost being to spiritual truth. On this second occasion she had again opened her vision; no one else but she could see that the Master was about to die; none of the others harboured such a thought, but Mary's inner self responded; seeing that he was about to depart from his friends, as a symbol of farewell she anointed his feet with the embalming oil. Mary understood the Master as none of the others did.

(12:9–15) *Much people of the Jews therefore knew that he was there: and they came not for Jesus' sake only, but that they might see Lazarus also, whom he had raised from the dead. But the chief priests consulted that they might put Lazarus also to death; Because that by reason of him many of the Jews went away, and believed on Jesus.*

On the next day much people that were come to the feast, when they heard that Jesus was coming to Jerusalem, Took branches of palm trees, and went forth to meet him, and cried, Hosanna: Blessed is the King of Israel that cometh in the name of the Lord. And Jesus, when he had found a young ass, sat thereon; as it is written, Fear not, daughter of Sion: behold, thy King cometh, sitting on an ass's colt.

In some schools of thought the ass is regarded as symbolical of the soul or psyche in man, which is the centre of desire, of feeling and emotion. Another symbol for the soul is that of the water, the soul can be turbulent as a rough sea, and needs to be controlled and subdued by the Christ (as Jesus demonstrated in the stilling of the waves). The unbroken ass which bore Jesus into Jerusalem stands for the soul or psyche which Jesus rode, proving that he was master of the emotional self (the ass) even as he proved master of the turbulent water. All men experience emotions and passions which rise up and overrule the judgment; man also knows that when the true spirit of Christ the Master arises within him these passions abate.

The crowd were ready to acclaim anyone who expressed material position and power but so rarely can they discern real merit and real spiritual greatness. They substitute fame and publicity instead. Jesus was trying to show the better way. He rode upon the ass, symbol also of humility. The crowd cheered him, but he was unmoved. The crowd is always ready to acclaim someone in high position, but fails to discern the true king.

(12 : 16–23) *These things understood not his disciples at the first: but when Jesus was glorified, then remembered they that these things were written of him, and that they had done these things unto him. The people therefore that was with him when he called Lazarus out of his grave, and raised him from the dead, bare record. For this cause the people also met him, for that they heard that he had done this miracle.*

The Pharisees therefore said among themselves, Perceive ye how ye prevail nothing? Behold, the world is gone after him.

And there were certain Greeks among them that came up to worship at the feast: The same came therefore to Philip, which was of Bethsaida of Galilee, and desired him, saying, Sir, we would see Jesus.

Philip cometh and telleth Andrew: and again Andrew and Philip tell Jesus. And Jesus answered them, saying, The hour is come, that the Son of man should be glorified.

The Son of man, we think, in this instance means the son of the flesh – or it denotes that etheric body of man which can be said to be born of the flesh (in a sense) because it shares the same vibrations as the body. Its lower part, which lingers for a short time after death of the physical body, and eventually, as we have said, disintegrates, is actually a replica of the physical body, but of a much finer texture. The purer part of the etheric body is that which will be saved to eternal life – that represents the Son of man. Jesus says the Son of man shall be glorified, inasmuch as spiritual life will infuse it and raise it to eternal life.

(12:24) *Verily, verily, I say unto you, Except a corn of wheat fall into the ground and die, it abideth alone: but if it die, it bringeth forth much fruit.*

The bodily self is the husk which will have to fall away, but inside is stored life; if the outer husk does not open the inner life must also die. In other words man must die to the world before he can be raised to eternal life. All lower desires and feelings must die. They do eventually; but while man clings to them he is himself as one dead. It is necessary to lose mortal shackles in order to gain spiritual wings.

When a soul passes to the spirit world, it comes burdened with its former self and is still of the earth, earthy; then it undergoes a wonderful spiritual experience while apparently still sleeping; when it eventually awakens to the true life, it becomes aware of an omnipresent God – God in all life, in the flowers, the trees, in the air it breathes, the running water, in the substance of the earth itself; God in the brother by his side, God in all form, God everywhere. Yet to reach this realisation the soul has had first to be severed, apparently from all earthly ties; to be willing to give up all for the supreme love of God. Yet in the very act of surrender, all is restored, because the soul is reborn into God's life; he sees his nearest and dearest in greater light and beauty than ever before, and they are restored to him, not in their lower self but as pure souls. In shedding the mortal life, which it once thought so precious, the soul has attained a life more abundant. You can never lose anyone dear to you for in love there can be no separation; there can be no loss to those who truly love.

(12:25) *He that loveth his life shall lose it; and he that hateth his life in this world shall keep it unto life eternal.*

When man is no longer dominated by the claims and passions of the body and of the lower self, he enters into the divine, he is reborn into a higher life. This can happen while still in the physical body; the soul surrenders desire only to be filled with intense enjoyment of the life more abundant; indeed this must come, for man is meant to enjoy all the gifts of God and to live every moment to express happiness.

(12:26–29) *If any man serve me, let him follow me; and where I am, there shall also my servant be: if any man serve me, him will my Father honour.*
Now is my soul troubled; and what shall I say? Father, save me from this hour: but for this cause came I unto this hour. Father, glorify thy name. Then came there a voice from heaven, saying, I have both glorified it and will glorify it again. The people therefore, that stood by, and heard it, said that it thundered: others said, An angel spake to him.

God's name is glorified by man made perfect, raised to perfection and eternal life by the Christ within him. The mystery we are endeavouring to teach is that man is glorified by the Christ spirit, and the purpose of man's life is that he shall glorify the flesh and glorify the earth, raise the vibrations of physical matter until the whole planet becomes etherealised and spiritualised and man returns again into the bosom of the Father Mother God.

(12:30–33) *Jesus answered and said, This voice came not because of me, but for your sakes. Now is the judgment of this world: now shall the prince of this world be cast out. And I, if I be lifted up from the earth, will draw all men unto me. This he said, signifying what death he should die.*

... Not by death of the spiritual life in him, but of that part of the etheric body which was earthy. The prince of this world – the body, the lower self. The spirit within shall grow so strong, so powerful that the body and the physical life no longer hold dominion. If I be lifted up – the Christ within be raised – I will draw all men unto me. True words, for with this upliftment of the Christ power within, man will worship by true motives, true thoughts, true action, and by example and power of his true self raise all about him.

(12:34–50) *The people answered him, We have heard out of the law that Christ abideth for ever: and how sayest thou, The Son of man must be lifted up? who is this Son of man?*

Then Jesus said unto them, Yet a little while is the light with you. Walk while ye have the light, lest darkness come upon you: for he that walketh in darkness knoweth not whither he goeth. While ye have light, believe in the light, that ye may be the children of light.

These things spake Jesus, and departed, and did hide himself from them. But though he had done so many miracles before them, yet they believed not on him: That the saying of Esaias the prophet might be fulfilled, which he spake, Lord, who hath believed our report? and to whom hath the arm of the Lord been revealed? Therefore they could not believe, because that Esaias said again, He hath blinded their eyes, and hardened their heart; that they should not see with their eyes, nor understand with their heart and be converted, and I should heal them. These things said Esaias, when he saw his glory, and spake of him.

Nevertheless among the chief rulers also many believed on him; but because of the Pharisees they did not confess him, lest they should be put out of the synagogue: For they loved the praise of men more than the praise of God.

Jesus cried and said, He that believeth on me, believeth not on me, but on him that sent me. And he that seeth me seeth him that sent me. I am come a light into the world, that whosoever believeth on me should not abide in darkness. And if any man hear my words, and believe not, I judge him not: for I came not to judge the world, but to save the world. He that rejecteth me, and receiveth not my words, hath one that judgeth him: the word that I have spoken, the same shall judge him in the last day. For I have not spoken of myself; but the Father which sent me, he gave me a commandment, what I should say, and what I should speak. And I know that his commandment is life everlasting: whatsoever I speak therefore, even as the Father said unto me, so I speak.

These last verses mean the same thing: the inner light in man can spiritualise and beautify the whole life. When the inner light is expressed in material life, down to the minutest detail of that life, God's will is being done, for God's will for man is perfection. This is the whole message of Christ – the manifestation of the light of heaven through earth. When the divine shines through the psyche it does not fade away with the physical body but is raised to eternal life; nor does the psyche have need for further incarnation because it has found its life in Christ.

It is most difficult to convey such truths in words. We have told you of what we have learned – that man has to be saved from his lower self and that that self has to die, for then the new man will be reborn into eternal life. That is what will come about in the new age – an expression, a manifestation in the world, of divine light. Then there will be no more death. To believe in and hope for a life after death is not enough. Man's soul must be reborn. For until a man is born again he cannot enter into the kingdom.

Men have studied the message of the Master Jesus, but they do not yet comprehend its full implication. Man does not even understand why his spirit came from realms of light as a divine spark, to dwell in matter. If man understood the purpose of his life here, instead of being bound down to earth he would turn his face thankfully to the light. Instead of dwelling on the form of the crucified man, he would see a risen Sun, and in the heart of that Sun he would see the Perfect One. He would see that form, with arms outstretched, making a cross of light within the circle of the light of the Sun, and he would be seeing his goal, the end of his travail.

Hold in your mind's eye this picture that we have drawn of Jesus, the Perfect One, standing with arms outstretched within the golden Sun. This golden Sun represents all life, for behind the physical Sun shines a spiritual glory which is its real life-essence and power. Every man or woman on earth has, deep within, this same light of the Sun (or Son), and, if he wills, may draw it to himself in ever increasing measure. He can absorb this life-force in the water he drinks, in the air he breathes, in the pure food he consumes. He can absorb this spiritual life-force in full consciousness, and it will cause him to grow in spirit until his whole being radiates the light as does that symbolic form of Jesus in the Sun – the picture of the risen Christ.

But something has to happen before man is resurrected from darkness to light, from death to life. When you live in the spirit, life is eternal; but the first step for man to take while on earth is to free himself from the bondage of his limiting flesh and to realise that it is his spiritual life which is real and eternal. In spirit there is no death, no separation; there is no time when you have not been, and there can be no time when you will not be. Sometimes we are asked, 'Shall we eventually be absorbed into the infinite light and glory of God, and so lose our individuality?' We say that as you develop and grow in the Christ life you will become even more and more individual, but at the same time become more and more absorbed into the infinite light you worship as God. Cannot you see that the more the Christ in man is developed, the more beautiful his form and life, the more certain it is that he will retain his individuality? The more certain also that, radiating the light of the Christ, he will become at one with the Father.

Jesus said: *I and my Father are one* (Jn. 10:30). He tried to teach the world the deep truth that God is within man. But man has been given freewill. He can allow God to develop, he can encourage the growth of Christ in him; or, by becoming immersed in his lower self, he can reject this very growth.

The story of the Christ birth and life, crucifixion, resurrection and ascension, is a symbolic presentation of the life of every man. Every event in the ordered life-story of Jesus of Nazareth is an initiation which will happen in each human life. Step by step the Master Jesus has shown how you, as a living soul, must traverse the path he trod; how, by a series of initiations (each initiation bringing an expansion of consciousness) you will advance along the spiritual path until you have finally overcome death, the last enemy of man.

The work of man's spirit here is so to purify the flesh that there is no disease, no corruption. The body is purified by the power of God within, so that when at death the lower form is shed, the form of the perfect one, the soul and the body of purified atoms, lives on, as Jesus demonstrated. As man purifies his life by divine love and wisdom, and by service to his brother man, so his physical body will become refined and rarified and his body will become so pure that it enters into the world of spirit without corruption of the flesh.

The Thirteenth Chapter

BETRAYAL AND FORGIVENESS

BEFORE resuming our subject we would speak of what may be looked for in a purified soul in an elder brother or master. Earthly people lack the power to see masters, and so they doubt their existence, but to the man or woman quickened by the light of the true spirit, recognition of purity and perfection in another becomes easier. Some of you may have had a vision on occasion of your guide or teacher, or of a beloved friend who has passed to a higher world; you will have been impressed by the beauty of that one, by the light radiating from him or her; there is a purity, a lightness; instead of fleshly heaviness, the spirit looks ethereal, as though illumined from some light within. With good reason you may believe that only beauty and peace encompass and fill the heart of your beloved in that life beyond. When a master or an elder brother manifests, a similar delicacy and purity about the very texture of his flesh can be noted.

Let us imagine that we are travelling along a lonely road over a mountain pass in, say, Tibet. In the distance a man approaches. At first we see nothing extraordinary, but as he draws nearer a change occurs within ourselves – we respond to certain emanations from him, and so are raised in consciousness, raised in understanding. Something is happening which we cannot quite define. As he draws closer still we see that he is no ordinary mortal. Light seems to stream from his eyes, his face and his whole body. The very texture of his flesh is different from that of an ordinary mortal – it is radiant, heavenly. Meditate on this picture, establish it through imagination until it becomes a living reality to you. You will know that holy man henceforth, and at any time can meet him in your meditation. His features may resemble those of a Tibetan, a Hindu, or an Englishman, or they may recall some well known painting of the Master Jesus.

He may even be an American Indian. Whatever facial form is his, you will recognise him by the heavenly purity of his form. You cannot mistake a master.

All this has a distinct bearing on the themes in this chapter of the gospel, in which Jesus is endeavouring to convey a vital truth concerning the psyche or soul of man, which is the bridge, the connecting link, through which pure spirit is enabled to manifest through a physical body.

The psyche, we again remind you, holds two aspects – that part which is of the earth and eventually disintegrates, and the other, the higher part which lives on to become eternal. This process of becoming eternal is slowly taking place through succeeding incarnations. As the soul or psyche is composed of these two parts, either of which can dominate, it can be either heavenly or the reverse. Much is absorbed into the psyche during successive incarnations; it is like a storehouse or repository for all the experiences of the earth. In the ordinary man it has not yet become purified, and is indeed the cause of much selfishness, greed, and desires, with which the higher self has to contend. This chapter deals with the need to purify the psyche – a very subtle lesson. The soul must become wholly pure and possessed of true humility and childlike simplicity. The Master said, *Except ye be converted, and become as little children, ye shall not enter into the kingdom of heaven* (Mt. 18:3). Unless the psyche becomes purified through acts of selflessness and love it cannot proceed very far, it cannot follow where the Master would go. Again, the Master said, *Whither I go, thou canst not follow me now* (Jn. 13:36), to which Peter answered *Lord, why cannot I follow thee now? I will lay down my life for thy sake* (37). The Master could see that Peter's psyche was far from being purified. He was like many who, although proclaiming themselves ready to renounce the world in order to follow the spiritual path, are not prepared to regard themselves as merely a channel or instrument, but still desire recognition and position. This is what the Master could see in Peter – an arrogance, a desire to be somebody of importance. But, 'No, Peter. Except you become as a little child, with a great love in your heart, not for yourself, not for the world, but for God alone, you cannot follow where I go'. Do you not see? Jesus was trying to teach the need for simplicity, the need to live a life which, though quiet and unnoticed, is like a healing spring of living water to the parched places.

What is the esoteric meaning, in this chapter, of Jesus washing the disciples' feet, and why did he indicate that if he washed Peter's feet there was no need for more? It is important, for, astrologically, the feet are associated with the water sign of Pisces, and Pisces is associated with the soul. Thus Jesus' washing the feet of the disciples was symbolic of purification of their psyche or desire body. He was teaching them that if the desires are pure there is no need to worry about anything else. This perhaps does not sound very important – but ponder on it; for once the psyche is cleansed, the desires pure, then thought and action are pure too.

This is what we meant in our little story about meeting the master in the mountains. The psyche of a master is freed from desire, is so purified that the very texture of the flesh is transmuted. The occultist refrains from eating meat or other coarsening foods, in order to hasten the purification of the physical vehicle. No doubt this helps – we think it does – but if the desires are pure it does not matter much what you eat, because the inflow of the pure waters of the spirit will cleanse and refine the physical atoms.

We then come to the episode of the betrayal of Jesus by Judas. Here is one of the most perfect examples of true brotherhood or divine love. It seems almost as if the Master selected Judas from among the disciples to betray him. You will remember that when they were gathered round the supper table he said, *one of you shall betray me*. At this the beloved disciple laid his head on the Master's breast. *Lord, who is it?* he asked. Here is an inference that Jesus deliberately chose his betrayer. Jesus said, *He it is, to whom I shall give a sop, when I have dipped it*. It was Judas. Jesus then said, *That thou doest, do quickly* (21–27). This again is curious. The Master knew that when an act is dwelt on in thought for too long many more implications will be drawn into the act itself. Many different threads or trivial events tend to centre around some big event. In working out karma many incidents seem to lead up to the actual happening. For this reason Jesus said to Judas, *That thou doest, do quickly*, because by meditating upon it Judas could have added to his load of karma. This brings up another point, for, on the spiritual path, the soul has to learn to take right action spontaneously. Until spiritual law has become so part of him that his spontaneous action and reaction is the right one, the soul will make mistakes. But it is better to make mistakes through impulse than by deliberate malice or evil thinking. Lessons can be learned through burning one's fingers.

Why did Jesus select Judas to betray him? This is a wonderful example of perfect love. Jesus was able to read far back into the past, and thus knew the karma which surrounded Judas. He saw that in the past Judas had once been a victim of betrayal and subsequent murder, and his instinct would be to repay that karmic debt by yet another betrayal and murder. Jesus knew that if Judas gave way to that instinct the karma thus set in motion between Judas and any ordinary man might continue through many lives to sway backwards and forwards, backwards and forwards. We once explained that the interplay of karma between souls might be likened to a ball tossed to and fro until such time as one soul returns good for evil. Herein we can read the true doctrine underlying the forgiveness or remission of sins. Jesus was remitting the sin of Judas. By his great love he drew that debt to himself so that he might forgive Judas, return love for hate, and thereby break a sequence which might have gone on for ages. Jesus would not repay evil with evil. He forgave the sin even before it had been committed, and thereby wiped it out. This same act of forgiveness is deeply embedded in the Master's teaching . . . forgive, forgive. Similar opportunities come to everyone; you can either return a forgiving love to one who has harmed you, or you can withhold that love and cherish a deep resentment which will later be worked out through the law of karma.

The concluding verses of the chapter contain the commandment to love one another. The Christ through the Master Jesus added: *By this shall all men know that ye are my disciples, if ye have love one to another* (35). The whole message of the great world teacher of the Piscean Age was of a divine love in which there can be no compromise. He meant what he said. He did not say, 'Love only in certain circumstances', but, *Love one another* (34) and *Bear ye one another's burdens* (Gal. 6:2). My brethren, the whole doctrine of Christ is that of brotherhood – and of the power of love. The two thousand years of the Piscean Age which have passed should be regarded as a period of preparation. In the age ahead, the Aquarian Age, mankind will be given new opportunities to put this teaching into action. It remains to be seen how quickly he will assimilate and understand the meaning of brotherhood and the power of love, how quickly he will learn to remit the sins of the world. When this happens we shall witness the second coming of Christ. Not through one divine man but through collective humanity will Christ express, through brotherhood and love, the way, the truth and the life. *And I, if I be lifted up from the earth, will draw all men unto me* (Jn. 12:32). The words mean no other than this.

(13:1–4) *Now before the feast of the passover, when Jesus knew that his hour was come that he should depart out of this world unto the Father, having loved his own which were in the world, he loved them unto the end. And supper being ended, the devil having now put into the heart of Judas Iscariot, Simon's son, to betray him; Jesus knowing that the Father had given all things into his hands, and that he was come from God, and went to God: He riseth from supper, and laid aside his garments; and took a towel, and girded himself.*

He laid aside his garments could be interpreted as meaning that he laid aside that heavenly life from which he had come. He was showing by symbol that he had come back to the world not by compulsion, for the completion of his karma, but voluntarily. He laid aside his clothing (his universal life) and girded himself with a towel – in other words he had put on mortal flesh, a human body. He took water (symbol of the psyche) and came to the world to help to purify man's soul from self and desire.

(13:5–10) *After that he poureth water into a basin, and began to wash the disciples' feet, and to wipe them with the towel wherewith he was girded. Then cometh he to Simon Peter: and Peter saith unto him, Lord, dost thou wash my feet? Jesus answered and said unto him, What I do thou knowest not now; but thou shalt know hereafter. Peter saith unto him, Thou shalt never wash my feet. Jesus answered him, If I wash thee not, thou hast no part with me. Simon Peter saith unto him, Lord, not my feet only, but also my hands and my head. Jesus saith to him, He that is washed needeth not save to wash his feet, but is clean every whit: and ye are clean, but not all.*

Peter had the aspiration, he wanted to be good, he wanted to follow the Master, but his desire body was not wholly clean, it was darkened with desires which none but the Master could see. Jesus wanted to cleanse Peter from this unworthiness. Peter wanted to shine before others. The Master then said to him, *The cock shall not crow, till thou hast denied me thrice* (38), thereby indicating that he knew the longing in Peter to stand well in the eyes of the world, and that Peter still lacked courage or strength to live bravely and humbly for the truth. How many are like Peter!

(13:11–16) *For he knew who should betray him; therefore said he, Ye are not all clean. So after he had washed their feet, and had taken his garments, and was set down again, he said unto them, Know ye what I have done to you? Ye call me Master and Lord: and ye say well; for so I am. If I then, your Lord and Master, have washed your feet; ye also ought to wash one another's feet. For I have given you an example, that ye should do as I have done to you. Verily, verily, I say unto you, The servant is not greater than his lord; neither he that is sent greater than he that sent him.*

If I then, your Lord and Master, have washed your feet; ye also ought to wash one another's feet (14). The Master meant this as a demonstration. In other words you must help your brother to cleanse himself of desire, do nothing to increase unworthy desire in him. This demonstration also shows the necessity for utter and complete humility. As Jesus said once before, *Not every one that saith unto me, Lord, Lord, shall enter into the kingdom of heaven; but he that doeth the will of my Father which is in heaven* (Mt. 7:21) – the soul that has become so purified of desire that it becomes unconscious of its own goodness. You do not tell by outward appearance or by a man's own words what he really is, but by his complete simplicity and humility. A great man or woman is truly humble, and rings true; he is unconscious of himself and is thus like a little child.

(13:17–31) *If ye know these things, happy are ye if ye do them. I speak not of you all: I know whom I have chosen: but that the scripture may be fulfilled, He that eateth bread with me hath lifted up his heel against me. Now I tell you before it come, that, when it is come to pass, ye may believe that I am he. Verily, verily, I say unto you, He that receiveth whomsoever I send receiveth me: and he that receiveth me receiveth him that sent me. When Jesus had thus said, he was troubled in spirit, and testified, and said, Verily, verily, I say unto you, that one of you shall betray me.*

Then the disciples looked one on another, doubting of whom he spake. Now there was leaning on Jesus' bosom one of his disciples, whom Jesus loved. Simon Peter therefore beckoned to him, that he should ask who it should be of whom he spake. He then lying on Jesus' breast saith unto him, Lord, who is it?

Jesus answered, He it is, to whom I shall give a sop, when I have dipped it. And when he had dipped the sop, he gave it to Judas Iscariot, the son of Simon. And after the sop Satan entered into him.

Then said Jesus unto him, That thou doest, do quickly. Now no man at the table knew for what intent he spake this unto him. For some of them thought, because Judas had the bag, that Jesus had said unto him, Buy those things that we have need of against the feast; or, that he should give something to the poor. He then having received the sop went immediately out: and it was night. Therefore when he was gone out, Jesus said, Now is the Son of man glorified, and God is glorified in him.

By the act of drawing to himself the karma of Judas, the soul of the Master became glorified in that it was manifesting divine love. When Christ is glorified in man it means that man is manifesting the glory of God. That is what happens when true forgiveness enters a man's heart, true love and understanding for one who has hurt him. Then God is being glorified. When God is glorified in man, God raises man and man is glorified in God. In other words, once a man forgives his enemy and loves him that same act so raises his soul in consciousness that it is linked directly to the Christ sphere and shares in the radiance of God's love. You may have experienced this in a small degree when you have returned love when you might have done the reverse. You are deeply, quietly, subtly happy. God glorifies Himself in you; He raises you up so that you share His happiness in heaven.

All these esoteric truths are for you, they are for every soul, and all are slowly moving upward on the mountain path. These things which we describe wait for every man in every age. Before you opens a path of ever-unfolding happiness, unbelievable to you as yet. We have described the appearance of a master, the beauty of his form, the purity of his soul; this is for you too. You will experience this, God will glorify himself in you, will manifest through you and thus you will be raised up. This is the path upon which your feet are set, and every effort of yours to love and to forgive is taking you higher, nearer to happiness and the perfecting of life.

(13:32–38) *If God be glorified in him, God shall also glorify him in himself, and shall straightway glorify him. Little children, yet a little while I am with you. Ye shall seek me: and as I said unto the Jews, Whither I go, ye cannot come; so now I say to you. A new commandment I give unto you, That ye love one another; as I have loved you, that ye also love one another. By this shall all men know that ye are my disciples, if ye have love one to another.*

Simon Peter said unto him, Lord, whither goest thou?

Jesus answered him, Whither I go, thou canst not follow me now; but thou shalt follow me afterwards.

Peter said unto him, Lord, why cannot I follow thee now? I will lay down my life for thy sake.

Jesus answered him, Wilt thou lay down thy life for my sake? Verily, verily, I say unto thee, The cock shall not crow, till thou hast denied me thrice.

You will see the insight of Jesus: *thou canst not follow me now; but thou shalt follow me afterwards* (36). Thou canst not come, yet; because Jesus could see the soul-karma and the desire body of Simon Peter and he knew he was unready, that this had to be cleansed before he would be ready to follow ... *but thou shalt follow me afterwards* – a promise that not only Peter, but all men shall attain to and enter the heaven prepared for them by the love of Christ the Son.

The Fourteenth Chapter

'THE FATHER IN ME'

AND SEEING *the multitudes, he went up into a mountain: and when he was set, his disciples came unto him: and he opened his mouth, and taught them* (Mt. 5:1–2). We are that multitude of listeners; we may also be disciples of Jesus, but whether or not we are disciples, we can still ascend the mountain of spiritual purity and aspiration, and listen in tranquillity of spirit to the voice of truth. Words cannot of themselves convey truth, but there are those around us, elder brethren, radiant, pure and holy spirits, angels from the throne of God, who can bring to each of you that sweetness, that love of the divine spirit, which will enable you to perceive truth and catch intuitively the underlying meaning of certain words or phrases. We meet as brethren, all on the same level, to listen to divine truth; we receive with you, and as we receive so we give. May peace dwell with each one.

The fourteenth chapter of the gospel is one of the most familiar chapters of all, and one that contains perhaps the jewel of the whole gospel, which can be summed up in that simple word, love – which is indeed the way, the truth and the life.

Spiritual truth is elusive and cannot always be clothed with words. It is not wise to try to understand this profound yet simple chapter with the intellect alone; only with development of the inner light will the meaning become clear. Only through a spirituality which is lived and expressed through warm and kindly human relationships (apart from any mental grasp of our subject) can the soul understand the profundity of Christ's teaching.

The letter killeth, but the spirit giveth life (2 Cor. 3:6). The letter of religion is killing religion. Only the spirit of love in the heart will give it life again. So long as religion deteriorates into an intellectual study it will lose its power, but when it becomes a

living force in the life of every individual soul then the world
will find salvation. This may sound old-fashioned but we mean
that the spirit alone gives life, eternal life. The light of the spirit
has become dimmed through man's descent into matter and
become clothed in self, but as a result of his experience and
suffering, it will grow in him till eventually it permeates every
walk of life.

The fourteenth chapter of St John reveals the true life the
world so sorely needs. It begins with the Master Jesus saying to
his disciples (and to all souls longing for truth and reality), *Let
not your heart be troubled: ye believe in God, believe also in me. In
my Father's house are many mansions* (1–2).

What is the meaning of *In my Father's house are many mansions*? 'In my Father's house', or home, we think refers to the
whole journey of the soul through many incarnations. In 'my
Father's house', in the life-journey which God has prepared for
the soul, are resting-places, are many mansions. These mansions
can be likened to states of consciousness, states of realisation,
times of illumination or perhaps initiation. In my Father's
house are many, many resting-places in which the soul receives
rest and refreshment – places which may be reached while still in
incarnation, or may be enjoyed in the world of spirit.

Let us bring this point home: you will know there are times in
your life when you go through difficulties, when life's journey
seems mostly uphill and you become weary and grimed with the
dust of everyday life and the sordidness of everyday conditions.
Unexpectedly you come across some resting place. You do not
know quite what happens; but one day, for no apparent reason,
you find yourself lifted up, and illumination and joy fill your
being. You have found one of the mansions of the Father
Mother God. Such demonstrations of the eternal and never failing love of God often go unrecognised, but nevertheless prove a
rich spiritual experience. When the Master speaks of
going to prepare a place for the disciple he adds, *if I go* (3)
meaning that the disciples will be greatly helped by his going.
His withdrawal from physical manifestation was to enable the

disciples to find the place they sought within their own consciousness. Whilst he was present with them they often failed to realise the truth of his words, but by his going he was preparing a place (or condition) wherein they might realise his continual presence with them and within themselves.

Sometimes you yourselves experience this. You listen to the voice of your guide or teacher and you are comforted. But then it seems that you are left apparently alone (in fact you are never left, although it may appear so) and then you have to make your own effort to reach the centre of truth and comfort. Did not the Master say, *Ask, and it shall be given you; seek, and ye shall find?* (Mt. 7:7). By experiencing periods of apparent aloneness the soul learns to ask and to seek, and through meditation and contemplation finds that a place in some higher state of consciousness has been made ready.

The trouble is that while the soul is imprisoned in a dense body it grows accustomed to thinking in terms of materialism; it cannot escape from the bondage of the flesh.

Later on Jesus speaks of the Holy Ghost, the Comforter, whom he should send, *even the Spirit of truth* (17). Throughout the centuries men have asked: What is this Holy Ghost? Who is the Holy Ghost? We can only endeavour to convey the idea in the following words: The Holy Ghost is the holy breath, the inbreathing of wisdom and of love. By the way you live, if you follow the example of Jesus, there will come to you this baptism, this inbreathing of the Holy Ghost; this is the initiation of the divine fire, the divine wisdom within. If it has lived the life as taught by Christ, when the soul turns to inward contemplation and meditation, the Holy Ghost enters it, and the holy breath or presence is felt, indescribable in words and which only the initiate knows and can understand. The Holy Ghost is a manifestation of the divine fire, the divine magic.

Let us go back to the time when Jesus was baptised by John in the river Jordan (Jn. 1:25–34) – baptised with water, symbolical of the cleansing and purification of his soul, of his preparation, or of his initiation into his mission, his period of service. The heavens opened and the dove descended from heaven, and rested upon the head of Jesus – a manifestation of the Holy Ghost, or of the divine Mother enfolding her Son, her beloved child, with the wisdom of the mother.

Think of the white dove as a manifestation of the Holy Ghost, which is also an aspect of the divine wisdom, the divine Mother, bearing within the creative fire of life.

For three years Jesus demonstrated to an ignorant humanity the powers of the Holy Ghost, of the divine fires which are the Holy Ghost.

You too can receive the Comforter, the baptism of divine fires. When this fire touches the upper chamber in your house, the highest centre in your head, it will bring a transmutation, it will bring wisdom, enabling you to loosen all bonds, and to reach the heights of universal wisdom wherein you will know all truth. Such a transmutation may be for a flash only at first, and a long time may pass before you again respond. But the process of evolution, of unfoldment and spiritual awakening and quickening goes ever forward, and you will, in due time, enter into complete understanding of the fires of the Holy Ghost, and of the creative powers within you, manifested long ago by Jesus, and which have been manifested since by others who have been baptised by the Holy Ghost.

(14:1–3) *Let not your heart be troubled: ye believe in God, believe also in me. In my Father's house are many mansions: if it were not so, I would have told you. I go to prepare a place for you. And if I go and prepare a place for you, I will come again, and receive you unto myself; that where I am, there ye may be also.*

Here is a transcendent thought: Although I go to prepare a place, I am sure to come again because I shall prepare this place within your consciousness by my going. Then we shall meet face to face. *That where I am, there ye may be also.* The soul that has touched the plane of Christ-consciousness is unified, at one with Christ. There can be no separation again.

(14:4–6) *And whither I go ye know, and the way ye know.*

Thomas saith unto him, Lord, we know not whither thou goest; and how can we know the way? Jesus saith unto him, I am the way, the truth, and the life: no man cometh unto the Father, but by me.

Notice that the disciples are continually thinking in material terms, but the Master speaks to them from the spirit. '*We* do not know the way, Master; *we* do not know where you will go' – they are speaking from the personal mind, which has to be laid aside before they can understand the esoteric significance of the Master's words.

I am the way, the truth, and the life: no man cometh unto the Father, but by me (6). These words contain the deepest truth! There have been teachers throughout the ages, great prophets who have contributed to man's progress along the pathway of evolution, but there is none greater than he. The light of Christhood is the illumination of the world. He is indeed the light of the world. Do not confuse Christ with the man through whom he worked. Jesus of Nazareth, the Initiate – the greatest initiate because he was able to renounce himself utterly and completely to the inflow of the divine light of Christ the Son. Jesus-hood is a state of progress, a condition to which all men will some day attain, a condition of purity, of perfectness, of perfected womanhood, perfected manhood. Christ-hood is that state of consciousness reached by the individual ego when it is ready to receive the illumination which is Christ, Son of the Logos, of the Father Mother God.

In Jesus we see the love and surrender to the will of the Father personified. *He that hath seen me hath seen the Father* because *I am in the Father, and the Father in me* (9–10). The mission of Jesus was to bring to humanity the teaching of love, because all human development, and development of the earth itself, is based upon that common denominator, love. His message was very simple: Love one another. Love is the fulfilling of the law, love in man's heart is his saving grace. It is not the man Jesus as a human being who saves the world, and yet he is the Saviour because through him flowed the heavenly light of the

Son, the supreme light of the heavens whom you know as Christ; and his was the example of divine love demonstrated in human life. *I am the way* (6) – the Son manifesting in human life as the light of the world. No man cometh unto the Father but by the way of absolute love.

(14:7–10) *If ye had known me, ye should have known my Father also: and from henceforth ye know him, and have seen him.*

Philip saith unto him, Lord, shew us the Father, and it sufficeth us.

Jesus saith unto him, Have I been so long time with you, and yet hast thou not known me, Philip? he that hath seen me hath seen the Father; and how sayest thou then, Shew us the Father? Believest thou not that I am in the Father, and the Father in me? the words that I speak unto you I speak not of myself: but the Father that dwelleth in me, he doeth the works.

Do you see the significance here? *If ye had known me, ye should have known my Father also* (7) – clearly indicating the inseparableness of the Trinity, the Father Mother God, and Christ the Son. A friend of ours was puzzled for a long time concerning the Trinity – which aspect was love, which aspect was wisdom. We answer, do not try to separate one aspect from the other. They are three in one and one in three. All three are love. Love is wisdom, wisdom is love, love and wisdom together are power. The Trinity of Father, Mother, Son is all love. God is love; and the manifestation of love in the life and works of His Son should teach you the nature of the Father. *Of myself I can do nothing, but the Father which dwelleth in me, He doeth the works* (10). It is the God in me (Jesus) which doeth the works, the healing, and which giveth truth in parables and teaching and performeth the miracles – all three aspects of the Trinity, love, wisdom and power, manifesting through this perfect man. What a divine heritage is ours! And how plainly Jesus points the way of life by *his* life – which must be our life, the only life. Unless this life is attained by and through a human personality the soul cannot live.

We have already said that the human psyche cannot truly live without union with the life of the Christ; and this brings us again to the profound mystery of the mystical marriage between the human psyche and the divine spirit. Saints and sages of all time have striven after this marriage, this union, this perfecting of the psyche, individuality or soul. Without the spirit of Christ the soul cannot attain eternal life. This is yet another interpretation of how Christ is the saviour of all mankind. If only we were sufficiently simple and humble to accept this vital truth, how quickly would man attain happiness and how soon would the golden age return!

The Father that dwelleth in me, he doeth the works (10): God is the power behind, who performs the healing, the miracles – not the personality of Jesus the Master, not even the Son, but God, the holy Trinity, doeth the works through the Son. But the Son is inseparable from God, for God is the Son and the Son is God.

(14:11–16) *Believe me that I am in the Father, and the Father in me: or else believe me for the very works' sake. Verily, verily I say unto you, He that believeth on me, the works that I do shall he do also; and greater works than these shall he do; because I go unto my Father. And whatsoever ye shall ask in my name, that will I do, that the Father may be glorified in the Son. If ye shall ask any thing in my name, I will do it. If ye love me, keep my commandments. And I will pray the Father, and he shall give you another Comforter, that he may abide with you for ever;*

Can you not see how wonderful and beautiful is this teaching? 'He will give you another Comforter' which will not depend upon any bodily manifestation of Jesus. The holy breath, the Holy Ghost, will enter your innermost being and its presence will be eternal. In a sense this is a promise to man's soul of union of his psyche or soul with the Spirit which gives it eternal life. Eternal life is something beyond survival of the human soul, a holy mystery brought about through the mystical marriage.

Whatsoever ye shall ask in my name, that will I do (13). People so often think they ask in the name of Christ, but in reality they ask for themselves. The law is that if a soul asks in the name of Christ, in the name of love, a manifestation of Christ in the life will follow. The difficulty is that often our prayers are egotistical. We must put aside self when we pray, for our prayers can only be fulfilled in the name of Christ.

(14:17–31) *Even the Spirit of truth; whom the world cannot receive, because it seeth him not, neither knoweth him: but ye know him; for he dwelleth with you, and shall be in you.*

I will not leave you comfortless; I will come to you. Yet a little while, and the world seeth me no more; but ye see me: because I live, ye shall live also. At that day ye shall know that I am in my Father, and ye in me, and I in you. He that hath my commandments, and keepeth them, he it is that loveth me: and he that loveth me shall be loved of my Father, and I will love him, and will manifest myself to him.

Judas saith unto him, not Iscariot, Lord, how is it that thou wilt manifest thyself unto us, and not unto the world? Jesus answered and said unto him, If a man love me, he will keep my words: and my Father will love him, and we will come unto him, and make our abode with him. He that loveth me not keepeth not my sayings: and the word which ye hear is not mine, but the Father's which sent me. These things have I spoken unto you, being yet present with you. But the Comforter, which is the Holy Ghost, whom the Father will send in my name, he shall teach you all things, and bring all things to your remembrance, whatsoever I have said unto you.

Peace I leave with you, my peace I give unto you: not as the world giveth, give I unto you. Let not your heart be troubled, neither let it be afraid. Ye have heard how I said unto you, I go away, and come again unto you. If ye loved me, ye would rejoice, because I said, I go unto the Father: for my Father is greater than I.

And now I have told you before it come to pass, that, when it is come to pass, ye might believe. Hereafter I will not talk much with you: for the prince of this world cometh, and hath nothing in me. But that the world may know that I love the Father; and as the Father gave me commandment, even so I do. Arise, let us go hence.

One more point: *If ye loved me, ye would rejoice, because I said, I go unto the Father: for my Father is greater than I* (28). Here is the gem of the whole, for it expresses the very essence of love, of brotherhood. To earthly people love usually means a desire for something, a drawing to themselves, a wanting to hold or possess this something or someone. The disciples did not want Jesus to go, they wanted to hold him. How many people would bind their loved ones to them if they could, and how few can rejoice at death! They do not know love when they feel bitter at the release of the soul from bondage, from darkness to light. True love, true brotherhood means becoming part of the life of the brother – being able to rejoice with another, entering into his joys and his sorrows. May these words comfort and inspire you when you are called upon to send forth the spirit of a loved one into the arms of God. Rejoice, and love. Forget all selfish desires, longing and pain and enter, in spirit, into the mansion which Christ has prepared for you and your loved one, in heaven.

Notice how much stress is laid upon the world being unable to understand. The world means that world of materialism, greed and selfishness, which does not know Christ. There is no room for him in that crowded feverish place.

Then Jesus says: *The prince of this world cometh* (30). Who is this prince? The prince of this world is death! Death and decay rule the world of matter. But the Master says that there is nothing in him that death can claim. Here is an interesting point which raises a big question, because the body of Jesus disappeared. While many suggestions have been made as to what happened to it there has never been an answer. Some say that the body of Jesus was caught up into heaven; but what happened to its physical atoms? It would seem from the words of the Master that no physical atoms remained – that they were transmuted into spiritual atoms. If this were so, then the prince of this world held no claim over the purified and perfected form of the Master, which was caught up into higher realms. Its physical atoms did not, could not decay – they became spiritualised.

The Fifteenth Chapter

'CONTINUE YE IN MY LOVE'

BRETHREN, the temple of truth is within your inmost being. To find truth you must leave outside all worldly cares, all material thoughts, and reverently enter the peace, the sweetness, the purity of the inmost court, the temple within yourself. Here shall be revealed mysteries which have existed through all time. Within will you find the key to all mysteries. There is no other way to truth. You can enter any temple or masonic lodge and pass through forms and ceremonies and prove no better spiritually, unless the heavenly grace descends upon you during that ceremony and becomes established in the inner lodge of your own being. But we shall hear more of this truth when we listen to the words of our beloved Master.

(15 : 1–27) *I am the true vine, and my Father is the husbandman. Every branch in me that beareth not fruit he taketh away: and every branch that beareth fruit, he purgeth it, that it may bring forth more fruit.*

Now ye are clean through the word which I have spoken unto you. Abide in me, and I in you. As the branch cannot bear fruit of itself, except it abide in the vine; no more can ye, except ye abide in me. I am the vine, ye are the branches: He that abideth in me, and I in him, the same bringeth forth much fruit: for without me ye can do nothing.

If a man abide not in me, he is cast forth as a branch, and is withered; and men gather them, and cast them into the fire, and they are burned. If ye abide in me, and my words abide in you, ye shall ask what ye will, and it shall be done unto you.

Herein is my Father glorified, that ye bear much fruit; so shall ye be my disciples. As the Father hath loved me, so have I loved you: continue ye in my love. If ye keep my commandments, ye shall abide in my love; even as I have kept my Father's commandments, and abide in his love. These things have I spoken unto you, that my joy might remain in you, and that your joy might be full.

This is my commandment, That ye love one another, as I have loved you. Greater love hath no man than this, that a man lay down his life for his friends. Ye are my friends, if ye do whatsoever I command you. Henceforth I call you not servants; for the servant knoweth not what his lord doeth: but I have called you friends; for all things that I have heard of my Father I have made known unto you. Ye have not chosen me, but I have chosen you, and ordained you, that ye should go and bring forth fruit, and that your fruit should remain: that whatsoever ye shall ask of the Father in my name, he may give it you. These things I command you, that ye love one another.

If the world hate you, ye know that it hated me before it hated you. If ye were of the world, the world would love his own: but because ye are not of the world, but I have chosen you out of the world, therefore the world hateth you. Remember the word that I said unto you, The servant is not greater than his lord. If they have persecuted me, they will also persecute you; if they have kept my saying, they will keep yours also. But all these things will they do unto you for my name's sake, because they know not him that sent me.

If I had not come and spoken unto them, they had not had sin; but now they have no cloke for their sin. He that hateth me hateth my Father also. If I had not done among them the works which none other man did, they had not had sin: but now have they both seen and hated both me and my Father.

But this cometh to pass, that the word might be fulfilled that is written in their law, They hated me without a cause. But when the Comforter is come, whom I will send unto you from the Father, even the Spirit of truth, which proceedeth from the Father, he shall testify of me: And ye also shall bear witness, because ye have been with me from the beginning.

Of all the chapters of the gospel, this seems best to summarise the meaning of all Christ's teachings. *I am the true vine* (1) means the I AM which we call Christ, not the Cosmic Christ only, but the Christ which dwells within every heart, the I AM being that divine love which can only speak within and from man's innermost sanctuary.

This life of Christ within you is a seed of the Cosmic Christ, a part of the true vine, and is the essence of all human consciousness and life. When man opens his innermost to this pure and gentle spirit of Christ he identifies himself with Christ. Therefore, being a branch of the true vine and himself living the Christ life, he must of necessity identify himself with all the feelings, joys and sorrows of his fellow man.

What does this mean to you personally? It means that in every detail you must enter into the life of your brother. Feel with him; know what he is going through, and think, 'how can I help him to bear his lot?'. Feel, live, love with your neighbour. Do not only regard him as some abstract 'Mr Smith' outside yourself but as a living being who is part of yourself. Try to identify yourself with him, with Christ, the spirit of God in him. Be thrilled with his joy, understanding of his sorrow. Talk to his heart, be gentle, kindly, sympathetic. Let your own heart lead you. A gentle word and feeling can often bring about a miracle. Live and breathe and serve your brother man in the spirit of true brotherhood, which is an over-all awareness of the at-one-ment of spirit, the harmony of all life.

This does not mean living the life of an ascetic, for if you live selflessly as a true son–daughter of God, you will live joyously. Nor is it a question of drawing your robes close about you and thinking you are wise and more advanced than others. It is a question of getting right down to basic things and feeling your at-one-ment with Mr or Mrs Smith, feeling as they feel, and instead of being egocentric, instead of being wrapped up in the meagre circle of personal interests, opening wide your windows and looking out upon the world with a great heart of sympathy and love. On the outer plane be quiet, watchful and understanding; in the inner temple let the light shine so that the motive behind every action and impulse is as pure, wise and loving.

131

Immediately man's spirit goes forth in adoration to God, his heart subtly contacts the rest of all creation, particularly the human creation. He realises in a flash his at-one-ment with God. He knows that if God is in himself, God is also in his brother man. If man finds God in the holy of holies within his own soul, he knows without being preached at that his fellow man has been created in the same way as himself, and shares in the same holy light. Even if it is unawakened, it is still there, waiting. And he knows that by giving out love to his neighbour he is not only helping his neighbour to deal with practical problems of daily life, but also to awaken to the eternal God-consciousness within him.

This is the meaning of the true vine – that man is part of the whole body of Christ.

The aim of every candidate for the mysteries is to become precise and perfect in daily life and in all human relationships. When you have achieved this you will not need to come to us again unless it is to talk over old times! You will yourself be the light, the perfect white brother.

Every branch in me that beareth not fruit he taketh away: and every branch that beareth fruit, he purgeth it, that it may bring forth more fruit (2). God prunes the vine. Beloved brethren, do you not know that all those ills from which you suffer, the disappointments, the sicknesses, the misjudgments, the grief and the pain – all these are the work of the wise pruner, that gardener who comes along and prunes the vine, removing unwanted branches to give strength and health to the tree. There are conditions to which you would cling if you could, but the wise pruner, the gardener knows that the tree must grow robust and strong, so he comes along and cuts out something which you would cling to. We from the spirit world would say, 'Do not cling to any outworn condition'. This may apply even to the passing of some dear one. You cry, 'Why, O why do I have to suffer this loneliness, this bitter bereavement?'. Of course, dear children, it seems very painful whilst you cling to the material and physical state. But as soon as you respond to the influence from that glorious world of light, of tranquillity and happiness, you are comforted, you are healed. You know then that all is good, that you yourself are growing in spirit towards consciousness of eternal and infinite life, of non-separation.

If a man abide not in me, he is cast forth as a branch, and is withered; and men gather them, and cast them into the fire, and they are burned (6). Whilst living in the body you are building up the psyche or soul with your emotions, good and otherwise. There are times when you feel like an outcast – that is to say, you are beset by thoughts of fear, anger, depression, anxiety. You seem to be in the outer darkness. While such emotions dominate, you are cut off from the true vine, from the source of life and strength. This separation manifests not only in the psyche but later in the physical body as well, for when the soul surrenders itself to violent emotions the true self becomes separated from the psyche of this incarnation. We will not go too deeply into this for we do not wish to disturb you; but when man's psyche becomes separated from the vine by inharmonious vibrations, emotions and dis-ease, the psyche of that incarnation can be cut off, wither and die, and be consumed in the fires. We are not preaching hell-fire; we merely speak of how a cosmic law operates. Very few people actually sink so low that their psyche is actually destroyed; but it can happen. When we speak of the psyche we mean at this moment only the personality which is being built up by the soul in the heavens, and which can be endowed with eternal life only through the indwelling Christ. We do not mean the spirit. In this sense Christ is the saviour of mankind. Without Christ the human psyche must die; with Christ, the human psyche is raised to eternal life.

If ye abide in me, and my words abide in you, ye shall ask what ye will, and it shall be done unto you (7). People sometimes say, 'My prayers are never answered so I don't pray any more'. Yet the Master, the Christ, very clearly states, *whatsoever ye shall ask of the Father in my name, he may give it you* (16). These words contain the secret of prayer and of true healing. There was once a woman who, having been assured that faith could move mountains, prayed that the mountain before her window should be removed. In the morning when she found the mountain was still there, she exclaimed, 'I thought as much!'. This story aptly defines the attitude of many people towards prayer. They pray without believing. We would not say that if you pray in faith that some hill which blocks your view will be removed, this will automatically happen. It is not enough to believe strongly; if we fail to identify ourselves with Christ we are still being selfish, putting our own self-will before the will of God. Such a prayer could never be fulfilled because it is not in accord with spiritual law. But if, when we pray, we identify ourselves into the law of love, the law of God, our prayer must be answered, because we are thus setting the law into motion. Prayer must be selfless and neither arrogant nor intolerant. Pray 'Lord, I accept Thy will knowing that what is good will be accomplished'. If without conflict or question we accept the works of God, we are surrendering to the law of love which was manifested through Jesus Christ. As an example of this form of prayer let us quote the incident when Jesus sorrowed in the Garden of Gethsemane. He did not pour forth bitterness or condemnation. He did not beg his Father to give him this or that. *O my Father, if it be possible, let this cup pass from me: nevertheless not as I will, but as thou wilt* (Mt. 26:39).

What must result from a prayer like this? It may not remove a hill or mountain, or provide the ideal companionship you want, or bestow material goods or restore the health that you think should be yours, but it will certainly raise you nearer to the Master and enrich your soul with a jewel of the spirit. Accept the cup, knowing that it is sent for God's wise and good purpose.

When you kneel to pray, whether you kneel physically or in spirit, you are performing a ritual. In the first place, to kneel affects the centres at the knees; the magnetism is stimulated and flows up through the body and helps in the opening of the crown chakra. Secondly, to kneel is an act of humility, of surrender.

So man kneels to pray, preparing himself both spiritually and physically to receive the blessing which can come when he has learnt to surrender all to God, saying 'Not my will but Thy will, O Lord'. Do you see the difference between this and demanding of God, 'I want this'? 'Do this for me, O God!' 'I want you to soften that person's heart.' In praying thus the individual is self-seeking – 'I want, I want, give me, give me'. *Ask what ye will, and it shall be done unto you* (7). It is true that when you earnestly pray you set in motion certain forces which can indeed direct things towards you. So a man has to learn to be very careful how he prays. Yes, 'ask and it shall be done unto you' – but first put yourself into the true attitude of heart and mind. When the soul can truly ask, not merely for itself, but that the will of God may be done on earth, in its life, it prays not for itself but for the blessing and the good of all mankind.

This true asking makes a direct, strong, clear contact with the source of all good. Those who are accustomed to meditate know that at a certain point in their meditation they can touch this source, this centre, a most ancient symbol of which is the dot within the circle, the symbol of the Sun (or the Son, the Christ, the child, the Son of God). When you truly pray, you touch that eternal centre, symbolised by the dot within the circle. This true contact, when you can make it, is most powerful, and has an effect both on yourself and those around you. You have asked for divine love, and it has been given, because you have asked in the right way.

There is an outer life of the world, and there is an inner life of the spirit. When you ask on the inner planes you will receive in full measure, and all your needs will be supplied, although perhaps not in the way you want or think they should be supplied. You must train yourself to seek only to fulfil the will of God, knowing that God is all-wise and loving, and that God will answer your prayer in the truest and finest way.

Being prepared to accept, accept, according to divine love, you have no need to doubt for one instant. Ask in the right spirit and the blessing will surely come. In this way mankind is reaching

upward to that state of mind and spirit where it knows at-one-
ment with infinite love, with the Cosmic Christ.

*As the Father hath loved me, so have I loved you: continue ye in
my love. If ye keep my commandments, ye shall abide in my love;
even as I have kept my Father's commandments, and abide in his
love. These things have I spoken unto you, that my joy might
remain in you, and that your joy might be full. This is my commandment, That ye love one another, as I have loved you. Greater
love hath no man than this, that a man lay down his life for his
friends. Ye are my friends, if ye do whatsoever I command you.
Henceforth I call you not servants; for the servant knoweth not
what his lord doeth: but I have called you friends; for all things
that I have heard of my Father I have made known unto you* (9–
15). Here Christ is identifying himself with humanity. *I call you
not servants . . . I have called you friends.* Is that not a beautiful
verse? Christ is raising humanity up to him. Remember he
said, *And I, if I be lifted up from the earth, will draw all men unto
me* (12:32). As man raises Christ in himself so Christ raises all
men. The whole of this gospel is trying to reveal the meaning of
identification of oneself with Christ. Christ here identifies himself with man. Man must therefore identify himself with his
brother man. In the degree he does this we see the spirit of
gentleness, brotherliness and kindness enriching all humanity.

Why does the voice of love speak so authoritatively, saying 'I
command'? For you will say, love does not command; but, you
see, the Christ in you can and does command when it is raised.
It commands love. In other words the Christ is the master, the I
AM in the soul. The true I AM commands all good, all health,
all harmony. It maintains control of all the vehicles – physical,
astral, mental, celestial. Christ rules all these bodies of man because he is supreme. The Christ within man rises in majesty,
claiming Sonship with God, his creator. *Ye have not chosen me,
but I have chosen you* (16). I have chosen, ordained you, given
you the power and the light, that ye may bear much fruit. What
a wonderful heritage is yours!

Ye have not chosen me, but I have chosen you, and ordained you, that ye should go and bring forth fruit, and that your fruit should remain: that whatsoever ye shall ask of the Father in my name, he may give it you. These things I command you, that ye love one another. If the world hate you, ye know that it hated me before it hated you. If ye were of the world, the world would love his own: but because ye are not of the world, but I have chosen you out of the world, therefore the world hateth you. Remember the word that I said unto you, The servant is not greater than his lord. If they have persecuted me, they will also persecute you; if they have kept my saying, they will keep yours also. But all these things will they do unto you for my name's sake, because they know not him that sent me. If I had not come and spoken unto them, they had not had sin: but now they have no cloke for their sin (16–22). If I had not given them light, if I had not spoken unto them, they would not have sinned because they would not have known. When knowledge comes, then there is sin; when there is ignorance there is no sin. Nevertheless this same life-force runs through the whole of mankind and reaches out to everyone – this wonderful love, this harmony, this oneness which makes each soul dependent upon the rest. So we may see a vast brotherhood of life all growing from the same stem, the true vine, all fed and watered by the same life-stream.

The Sixteenth Chapter

LIFE ETERNAL

SOME CONFUSION exists about what we mean by spirit, for the word can have more than one interpretation. When we speak of spirit we are not referring to the life-force which animates the physical body. This is not the life of the spirit, it belongs to the physical world. Life eternal is not of this world. *For the prince of this world cometh, and hath nothing in me* (14:30) – the ruler of the physical aspect of life has nothing in common with the divine essence in man which is pure spirit. When the physical life-force is withdrawn, the body dies; but when the pure spirit, love, the divine essence, is withdrawn, a kind of death takes place which operates on the psychic as well as on the physical plane.

When contemplating this sixteenth chapter we should get clearly in the mind the meaning of the pure spirit, the divine essence; which when withdrawn, all that remains is death. 'Rebirth' is usually taken to mean reincarnation; but there may also be a rebirth of the soul on to the plane of pure spirit – *except a man be born again* (3:3). Jesus said that such a rebirth could only come to his disciples by his withdrawal from their midst.

Let us consider what takes place when two people become separated through death. One continues to live in the world; the soul of the other goes onward. Sometimes a wonderful experience can befall the person left behind, for his soul may become raised in consciousness to the plane of spiritual life where the loved one now dwells. Some of you may have experienced this true communion through at-one-ment, or attunement of spirit. Or it may be that in the quiet of meditation you have touched for a flash (you could not hold it for long) the cosmic or the Christ-consciousness, and become aware of the plane of pure spirit. No one who has experienced this can ever forget it.

This Jesus had in mind when he spoke to his disciples about the necessity for his departure before they could receive the spirit of truth, the Comforter. He knew that they were clinging to his bodily presence, and while they were clinging to the bodily presence they could not experience that rebirth into cosmic or Christ-consciousness, that spiritual renewal which could only come to them by his withdrawal.

Jesus often talked with his disciples, for many of them had been with him a long time, and he knew that much of what he said was only understood intellectually as far as they were concerned; it had yet to become part of them. There is a vast difference between merely knowing things with the mind, and knowing them with the deep understanding of the heart – or, in other words, welcoming into the soul the divine breath which is pure love and wisdom. The spirit of truth being itself the Comforter cannot be received or welcomed by the soul until it has learned to respond to the impetus of a love so strong that the soul can only spontaneously give and give. Did not the saints live thus, without thought for themselves? The return for truly loving is the gift of that spirit of truth which brings life, not death; and it brings power also.

You will now recognise how necessary it was for Jesus to withdraw in order that the great love he had inspired in the disciples would lift them towards him, towards cosmic consciousness; and would urge them to love and to give to the world as he had given. But their urge thus to help mankind would not awaken while he was there with them. He had to withdraw ere they could receive the spirit and manifest its power.

It is natural when living in a physical body to think, even unconsciously, that bodily things are the most important; even those who know something concerning spiritual matters still tend to put things of the world first. In a way they are right: the physical life is important because only experiences in earth can quicken the breath of life in the soul. The ideal is to correct our perspective, to realise that physical life forms only a part of life, not the whole. Moreover, physical life is not eternal. The body can die, but the divine spirit can impregnate the soul – the soul that man creates for himself out of his own desire nature – so that it lives eternally.

The purpose of your life is that you may learn to live in the spirit, and that the divine breath or spirit may live in you, in matter; and that as you climb the arc of life, you may take with you an individualised soul, grown pure and eternal, and so enter the kingdom of heaven as a living soul.

When Jesus said to his disciples, *Whither I go, thou canst not follow me now* (13:36), what did he mean? Those who believe simply in life after death are puzzled, for if he referred to the spirit world they know that all must in due course follow him. But remember that he could see into the minds of his disciples and knew that much of his teaching was only intellectually understood. Therefore he knew that until something happened to awaken them to the reality of pure spirit they could not follow where he went. He was about to return to the plane of spirit, to his Father; they were not yet clothed to meet the heavenly bridegroom.

The same meaning lies in the parable of the guest who was not fittingly robed for the wedding feast. That clothing symbolises a soul impregnated with the life and the love and the truth of pure spirit. Such a spirit wears a robe of scintillating and sparkling light, and this is its wedding garment. It is one matter to know spiritual truth intellectually and quite another to be clothed in spiritual truth so that every thought and word and act is a spontaneous expression of divine love and light.

You may protest that it is not possible to live thus on earth. We know your difficulties; but we are also sure that an effort must be made. You must keep trying, and be steadfast in your effort, realising that if you can express for one flashing moment that spontaneous love, you will have taken a momentous step forward.

This truth you will find repeated again and again in the gospel of St John in such statements as *I am the true vine* (15:1); *I and my Father are one* (10:30). Man must realise both whence he comes and whither he goes before he can find any sense in life; otherwise he veers about like a rudderless ship. Once man recognises his captain, once that captain takes command, true joy replaces travail and sorrow, because the soul can at last understand that in order to create and build itself anew it may have to undergo certain experiences which will draw to it some of those finer elements from heaven to be built eternally into the soul body. Sorrow can do this, and joy also.

(16:1–9) *These things have I spoken unto you, that ye should not be offended. They shall put you out of the synagogues: yea, the time cometh, that whosoever killeth you will think that he doeth God service. And these things will they do unto you, because they have not known the Father, nor me. But these things have I told you, that when the time shall come, ye may remember that I told you of them. And these things I said not unto you at the beginning, because I was with you. But now I go my way to him that sent me; and none of you asketh me, Whither goest thou? But because I have said these things unto you, sorrow hath filled your heart. Nevertheless I tell you the truth; It is expedient for you that I go away: for if I go not away, the Comforter will not come unto you; but if I depart, I will send him unto you. And when he is come, he will reprove the world of sin, and of righteousness, and of judgment: Of sin, because they believe not on me;*

When truth comes into a man's heart he sees with very different eyes. His values change. He becomes able to discern the things of the spirit. When the spirit of truth wakes in a man he sees beneath the surface of things, the reality within the outer semblance, and no longer needs the judgment of the world as his guide.

(16:10–11) *Of righteousness, because I go to my Father, and ye see me no more; Of judgment, because the prince of this world is judged.*

When the spirit of truth comes the world is at once judged,

because the soul can now discern the real from the unreal, the false from the true.

(16:12–13) *I have yet many things to say unto you, but ye cannot bear them now. Howbeit when he, the Spirit of truth, is come, he will guide you into all truth: for he shall not speak of himself; but whatsoever he shall hear, that shall he speak: and he will shew you things to come.*

There are things I cannot tell you because you are not ready. Something has to be undergone before the soul is open to receive truth – maybe a great sorrow or great joy must be experienced. Something has to crack the shell, or break the crust.

(16:14–18) *He shall glorify me: for he shall receive of mine, and shall shew it unto you. All things that the Father hath are mine: therefore said I, that he shall take of mine, and shall shew it unto you. A little while, and ye shall not see me: and again, a little while, and ye shall see me, because I go to the Father.*
Then said some of his disciples among themselves, What is this that he saith unto us, A little while, and ye shall not see me: and again, a little while, and ye shall see me: and, because I go to the Father? They said therefore, What is this that he saith, A little while? we cannot tell what he saith.

The disciples had yet to receive the spirit of truth, or understanding. Therefore Jesus said: *A little while, and ye shall not see me* (16), because they will then be going through a period of darkness. Later on, when they have had their experience (and this applies to all of you) they will awaken and be ready to follow the way of Christ. It is a stage of unfoldment of the soul of man.

(16:19–22) *Now Jesus knew that they were desirous to ask him, and said unto them, Do ye enquire among yourselves of that I said, A little while, and ye shall not see me: and again, a little while, and ye shall see me? Verily, verily, I say unto you, That ye shall weep and lament, but the world shall rejoice: and ye shall be sorrowful, but your sorrow shall be turned into joy. A woman when she is in travail hath sorrow, because her hour is come: but as soon as she is delivered of the child, she remembereth no more the anguish, for joy that a man is born into the world. And ye now therefore have sorrow: but I will see you again, and your heart shall rejoice, and your joy no man taketh from you.*

You pass through sorrows which you feel you can never get over; it is as though you undergo the travail of birth, but as a result of your bitter travail a new and deeper understanding is born, and great joy.

(16:23) *And in that day ye shall ask me nothing. Verily, verily, I say unto you, Whatsoever ye shall ask the Father in my name, he will give it you.*

Then there will be nothing left to ask for. The soul of the disciple on that day will be complete, it will know truth. Possessing all truth within itself, it will not have to seek further.

(16:24–33) *Hitherto have ye asked nothing in my name: ask, and ye shall receive, that your joy may be full. These things have I spoken unto you in proverbs: but the time cometh when I shall no more speak unto you in proverbs, but I shall shew you plainly of the Father. At that day ye shall ask in my name: and I say not unto you, that I will pray the Father for you: for the Father himself loveth you, because ye have loved me, and have believed that I came out from God. I came forth from the Father, and am come into the world: again, I leave the world, and go to the Father.*

His disciples said unto him Lo, now speakest thou plainly, and speakest no proverb. Now are we sure that thou knowest all things, and needest not that any man should ask thee; by this we believe that thou camest forth from God.

Jesus answered them, Do ye now believe? Behold, the hour cometh, yea, is now come, that ye shall be scattered, every man to his own, and shall leave me alone: and yet I am not alone, because the Father is with me. These things I have spoken unto you, that in me

*ye might have peace. In the world ye shall have tribulation: but be
of good cheer; I have overcome the world.*

The soul born of the Christ enters into a peace which passes
all understanding, into a truth beyond all worldliness. This
peace, this truth and this life Jesus was teaching his disciples
how to find. So it is happening with you also. Those who have
truly seen and entered into the kingdom know only peace.
Nothing can disturb them – no fears, no tribulations. The
soul who knows, dwells in Christ and in the Father, and enjoys
the peace of a soul reborn to the life of divine spirit.

This whole chapter describes the path of the neophyte, and
indicates the meaning of the soul being initiated into the Christ
state. It describes the experiences which every soul must
undergo before it can pass through the gates of initiation. It
emphasises the importance of the real life of spirit (and the *living*
of that life) as against the insignificance of material existence. It
also guides the disciple to interpret every experience and every
act in terms of the spirit. The disciple should always look for an
inner meaning, the life within the outer form, yes, even of the
very food he eats or the clothing he wears; and the trivial things
of every day. Behind and within all, is spirit. Do not cast aside
the outer, physical life, for it grows more important, and takes its
true place, when lived with understanding of spiritual values.
Everything you do in the outer world should be a spontaneous
manifestation or expression of the spirit.

We have endeavoured to give in broad outline the inner meaning of this chapter. The truths taught long ago by Jesus and so
beautifully recorded by St John are still waiting to be understood and lived, as they have not been lived and understood
before, except by the saints, and even some of these have been
limited by the day in which they lived. Now we are coming into
the new age, when the teachings of St John will be the foundation of a new church, but not a church such as you know today.
The church of St John will be built into men's lives, into men's
hearts, into men's souls. Man will learn to worship in his own

temple, in the sacred place of his own heart. He will not live by physical values only, but by the light of his spirit, which will show him how to behave towards his fellows. There will be no need then for social legislation. The foundations of the church of St John will be pure spirit, for the temple will rise out of the kindliness of men's lives. On earth will come a perfect brotherhood. Then men will no longer worship Mammon. The prince of this world will recede before the spirit of love and brotherhood.

The Seventeenth Chapter

'GLORIFY THOU ME'

WE TRY to express in language of earth a love which is divine and beyond all expression through words. We ask you to open your hearts and listen to the silent voice of truth within. We would raise you into heavenly spheres of life so that you can see the company about you. Imagine (if you like to use that much misused word) that you are far away from the earth, in a temple, lofty, wide, long, and blazing with spiritual light, giving the impression of a temple of pure gold. See the white-robed brethren – beautiful forms, beautiful faces. With each brother you know that you look upon the face of one who is wholly good, loving, true and powerful – a face illumined with the light of the spirit of goodness, of God. These are your brethren, your guides and your inspirers.

Yet man turns away from such company to the turmoil and strife of earth, an earth which should be so beautiful but which has been desecrated by the passion and selfishness of man. Do you wonder then why we of the brotherhood come back to the earth endeavouring to thin the veil between the world of spirit and the world of matter? For we have seen and know what awaits the sons of God if only they will turn their faces towards the light!

This needs more than an intellectual understanding, although the intellect can be used by the spirit to help man to comprehend the truths of eternity. But the simple human soul, the kindly loving heart, can best understand truth; can more easily rise on wings of light beyond the shadowed earth into the heights where these temples of the brethren of the light are built from the etherealised substance of life. The physical eye cannot see; but when the vision is true and sure all men will behold the glories which God has prepared for those that love Him, for every soul which lives in harmony, quietly and tranquilly, in peace and

goodwill towards others. These are they who of their own voli-
tion can behold the vision beautiful, and it is to these the messengers come. It is for those who live lovingly to teach those who
still slumber – as the angel once woke the sleeping shepherds – to
behold the glory in the heavens. This same glory is that which
the beloved Master was about to enter when he spoke of going to
His Father in heaven that he might be perfected; and when he
said: *And I, if I be lifted up from the earth, will draw all men unto
me* (12:32).

He spoke so forcibly of the need for him to leave the earth
before he could truly raise his brethren, for while he dwelt
among them they clung to him. Only by going forward into the
light could he rouse those who slept – only in this manner could
they learn of the brotherhood of the spirit.

We touch on this because we hope to give some fleeting idea
of truth which may in time quicken your understanding. In the
heavens are what might be called temples of initiation, but which
more accurately are planes or higher levels of knowledge and
truth which the incarnate soul of man is enabled to reach on
occasion. We have spoken of this before. When the soul undergoes some deep emotional experience, when it is called upon to
face major difficulties and problems, it sometimes prays to God
for help; and then a messenger, a brother of the light from the
temple above, comes to the soul of the man or woman who thus
calls to God; and this messenger draws the suppliant into his
aura and raises him, so that almost unconsciously his soul is
lifted above darkness, fear, sorrow and worry. A deep inward
calm prevails. The soul has undergone a form, a ritual, a profound spiritual experience in a lodge above. When it returns it
brings back more knowledge, a jewel of spiritual light.

You may regard your neighbour as an ordinary-enough
person. But we tell you truly that every man and woman, even
the least, has another part of himself or herself which the world
cannot see; and often that other self is clothed in shining raiment
and wears a jewel upon its breast. Who dares to judge the soul of
any man by earthly valuation?

What impulse then, causes the soul to long to journey upwards, even while still imprisoned in the flesh? It is the indwelling flame of Christ ... something indescribable which Christ has transferred to man. When we speak of Christ, remember that we do not mean Jesus Christ only. Were this so, what of the millions who lived before Jesus was born? By Christ we mean the spirit of love, truth and power dwelling in the heart and centre of every man. Only that spirit or that light within can raise you to the temple above and so expand the consciousness that you can see things in a pure, clear light. This only comes about when you allow the Christ within to raise you to the heavenly places.

We will now turn to what St John says concerning the going forth of the Christ spirit which spoke through the soul or personality of Jesus. Think about what we have been saying as you read the words.

(17:1–26) *These words spake Jesus, and lifted up his eyes to heaven, and said, Father, the hour is come; glorify thy Son, that thy Son also may glorify thee: As thou hast given him power over all flesh, that he should give eternal life to as many as thou hast given him. And this is life eternal, that they might know thee the only true God, and Jesus Christ, whom thou hast sent. I have glorified thee on the earth: I have finished the work which thou gavest me to do. And now, O Father, glorify thou me with thine own self with the glory which I had with thee before the world was.*

I have manifested thy name unto the men which thou gavest me out of the world: thine they were, and thou gavest them me; and they have kept thy word. Now they have known that all things whatsoever thou hast given me are of thee.

For I have given unto them the words which thou gavest me; and they have received them, and have known surely that I came out from thee, and they have believed that thou didst send me.

I pray for them: I pray not for the world, but for them which thou hast given me; for they are thine. And all mine are thine, and thine are mine; and I am glorified in them. And now I am no more in the world, but these are in the world, and I come to thee.

Holy Father, keep through thine own name those whom thou hast given me, that they may be one, as we are. While I was with them in the world, I kept them in thy name: those that thou gavest me I have kept, and none of them is lost, but the son of perdition: that the scripture might be fulfilled.

And now come I to thee; and these things I speak in the world, that they might have my joy fulfilled in themselves. I have given them thy word; and the world hath hated them, because they are not of the world, even as I am not of the world. I pray not that thou shouldest take them out of the world, but that thou shouldest keep them from the evil. They are not of the world, even as I am not of the world.

Sanctify them through thy truth: thy word is truth.

As thou hast sent me into the world, even so have I also sent them into the world. And for their sakes I sanctify myself, that they also might be sanctified through the truth. Neither pray I for these alone, but for them also which shall believe on me through their word; That they all may be one; as thou, Father, art in me, and I in thee, that they also may be one in us: that the world may believe that thou hast sent me. And the glory which thou gavest me I have given them; that they may be one, even as we are one: I in them, and thou in me, that they may be made perfect in one: and that the world may know that thou hast sent me, and hast loved them, as thou hast loved me.

Father, I will that they also, whom thou hast given me, be with me where I am; that they may behold my glory, which thou hast given me: for thou lovedst me before the foundation of the world. O righteous Father, the world hath not known thee: but I have known thee, and these have known that thou hast sent me. And I have declared unto them thy name, and will declare it: that the love wherewith thou hast loved me may be in them, and I in them.

Notice the reference to Christ and the Father being together before the foundation of the world. This would indicate that before humanity came into being, this spirit of the Son (or of

love) coexisted with the Father, forming the holy Trinity of
Father Mother Son; and that the world and all creatures dwelling upon earth came forth from the blessed and holy Trinity.
The spirit of the Son was to descend to bless, to take form, as
the highest creature, man; the Son was destined to manifest the
glory of the Father through man.

Within humanity two aspects of the cosmos are manifest – the
world, the lower self, on the one hand, and the spirit of the Son
or Christ on the other. Only through manifestation of the love of
the Son in man by man can he be saved from destruction.

Then Jesus speaks of the 'son of perdition', saying that none
will be destroyed save he. This reference is usually thought to
refer to Judas. We would put the story in a different light and
suggest that the 'son of perdition' really represents some quality
inherent in the soul of every man, which is responsible for all
that is negative and destructive. Nevertheless this quality (which
has its part to play in stimulating and strengthening that which
is good and of the light), because it originates from darkness and
evil, must surely bring about its own destruction. It is said that
after Judas had done his work he destroyed himself. Cannot you
see the symbolism in this? Of course the 'son of perdition'
housed in Judas must consume itself, for the evil in man is ever
self-destructive and must indeed be 'consumed in the fires'.
That which caused Judas to betray his Master could have no
other end, for that is the law.

This chapter is beautiful in its apparent simplicity – once you
have the key. Without the Christ aspect there is nothing in man
for man to live for; in the world nothing endures but that which
comes into life by power of the Father and the Son. Jesus prayed
that the Father would glorify him and give him power to raise
his disciples – men lately awakened. Aware of the limitations
which beset the human soul he knew that only the glory of God
manifesting through him, Jesus the man, could reach those disciples. Here the gospel states clearly that man must respond to
that Christ spirit, else he is dead. In a lesser degree, we too (all of
us) are, in a sense, saviours of our brothers: if we live, as Christ

taught us to live, a life of utter love, gentleness, simplicity and tenderness. In this way the Son, the Christ, uses us, and we are saviours of our brother.

This brings us back to the doctrine of brotherhood and good-will. Only through aspiring to the Father could Jesus become one with the Father, and only through that at-one-ment could he save his brethren on earth. This, the whole chapter teaches, that there is only one way of life, the Christ way. Then Jesus indicates that he has given all that he can give while in the flesh. Now he must return to the temple above and from there direct – shall we say the salvation of man's soul? It was necessary for him to lay aside the body which had served him and to become pure spirit in order to accomplish this further work – and his work, he clearly said, henceforth would be in the heavens or from the heavens.

We have come back in a circle to where we explained how the soul could leave its sleeping body and be drawn up to the temple above; and that there the work of Christ continued. So we see that the spirit of Christ, the Son, must live in heavenly glory and at appointed times pour down streams of love and light so that Christ may raise all men towards his heart of love in heaven above.

These words spake Jesus, and lifted up his eyes to heaven, and said, Father, the hour is come; glorify thy Son, that thy Son also may glorify thee: As thou hast given him power over all flesh, that he should give eternal life to as many as thou hast given him. And this is life eternal, that they might know thee the only true God, and Jesus Christ, whom thou hast sent (1–3). Life eternal does indeed come to the soul who sees Christ, who understands the love of the Father. He lives thereafter by the love of the Father and of the Christ; for love is life, and lack of love spells death.

Jesus came to manifest the glory of God in his nature, in his presence and in his life. Having *finished the work which thou gavest me to do* (4), which was to glorify God through the form of man, he returned to his Father. Any man who is perfected, that is to say who has finished the work which the Father gave him to do, any soul which has passed through numberless incarnations and has triumphed over the world, returns to the heavens and has no need to come into incarnation again, having already manifested the glory of God.

And now, O Father, glorify thou me with thine own self with the glory which I had with thee before the world was (5). A new life is prepared for every soul that accomplishes the work of God while in the flesh, and every soul will accomplish this in course of time. The ultimate goal of every soul is the heavenly blessedness of union with God. In this heavenly union identity will not be lost, for in union with God the soul becomes at one with all. Many think that the Nirvana of the Buddhists and the heaven of the Christians implies a kind of annihilation or extinction of the individual soul, but this is not so. It means the perfecting of each soul so that it enters into absolute at-one-ment with life and with God. Henceforth, no disruptive note mars the harmony of the soul. What a life that will be for all of us who have still to be about our Father's business on earth!

I have manifested thy name unto the men which thou gavest me out of the world: thine they were, and thou gavest them me; and they have kept thy word. Now they have known that all things whatsoever thou hast given me are of thee. For I have given unto them the words which thou gavest me; and they have received them, and have known surely that I came out from thee, and they have believed that thou didst send me (6–8). This does not refer only to the twelve disciples but to all men and women who have arrived at that point on the path, on the journey back to God, at which they can see Christ revealed in the hearts of men and in all life. Every soul will ultimately reach the point where it can recognise truth instantly.

And now I am no more in the world, but these are in the world, and I come to thee. Holy Father, keep through thine own name those whom thou hast given me, that they may be one, as we are. While I was with them in the world, I kept them in thy name: those that thou gavest me I have kept, and none of them is lost, but the son of perdition; that the scripture might be fulfilled. And now come I to thee; and these things I speak in the world, that they might have my joy fulfilled in themselves. I have given them thy word; and the world hath hated them, because they are not of the world, even as I am not of the world. I pray not that thou shouldest take them out of the world, but that thou shouldest keep them from the evil. They are not of the world, even as I am not of the world (11–16). Jesus the Christ understands how hard things can be for those who follow the path. He knows how much they need the love and protection of God. Some people seem to think that it is easy for others to be good, because the way of the flesh fails to tempt them. But those who think thus fail to understand how difficult it is for any soul to keep to the true and righteous path, and harder still for those who reach the high places, where temptations grow more subtle and greater can be the fall (a lesson which was taught in the temptations in the wilderness). Jesus knew that the disciple is in even greater need of the spiritual help of the Father than the unawakened. He speaks tenderly in this chapter of you; it is for you that this message comes. Jesus is speaking to you individually, knowing, sympathising with your difficulties, mistakes and failures. He prays to the Father to give you ever more help as you climb the path.

Sanctify them through thy truth: thy word is truth. As thou hast sent me into the world, even so have I also sent them into the world. And for their sakes I sanctify myself, that they also might be sanctified through the truth (17–19). The Master is teaching the lesson of brotherhood the whole time. It is the law of brotherhood that the one above always reaches a hand down to help the one below. But although we in spirit always grasp the hand of those still on earth we have our other hand in that of an angel above. And while we look up, we also guide those below. All love is like that. Here we find love perfectly expressed in action. Here may be an answer to those who say 'why dabble with spirits?' This is the reason. Consciously or unconsciously man has a hand in the hand of his guide above, and must reach up to receive the help he craves.

The Eighteenth Chapter

THE ACT OF SURRENDER

TO UNDERSTAND the truths of spirit it is necessary to rise above the limitations of earthly thought and intellectual conceptions, for man cannot grasp spiritual truth with his intellect alone. As Jesus himself taught, only the childlike in heart can enter the kingdom. At the present time particularly so many grievous and complex problems await solution, and men and women look in vain to their leaders for answers to their questions; but until he himself has entered the kingdom of truth he cannot answer the child of earth. The great brotherhood draw very close to men to bring them enlightenment about how to live according to the law of God; but mankind has become absorbed in the density of materialism and materialistic thought and it is not easy to penetrate this dense veil.

It is so long since the Master spoke to his children some feel his teaching to be impractical for this age; others still hope that their Lord will return in all his glory, accompanied by angelic hierarchies. So materially-minded has man become that he expects to see with physical sight the coming of the Lord. Man lies sleeping in materialism, but God the almighty spirit uses many ways to arouse him from this deathlike sleep. Sometimes this quickening will take the form of personal loss, sorrow or suffering. God moves in a mysterious way to perform his wonders in the material life, as your own experience has probably taught you.

The miracles of the Master Jesus were not confined to the period of his ministry on earth, but are still being performed among men. Many, failing to recognise this fact, do not realise that what they undergo through sickness, sadness, sorrow, or loss of position or material wealth, comes to them as an act of God designed to quicken their spirit. Only when the spirit within man is awakened can he behold the coming of the Master in the

silence of his innermost being. The second coming will not be an
outward but an inner manifestation. Christ and the Christ-circle
are waiting for your hour of quickening, so that you may open
your inner eyes to see his glory, and become aware of his power
to rule your life.

This preamble, you will find, is directly related to the eighteenth chapter of the gospel, which clearly states that the kingdom of heaven is the kingdom of love and truth; and that the
ministry of the Master Jesus was destined to bring to mankind
this vision of the true kingdom. Did not he teach his disciples to
pray, *Thy kingdom come. Thy will be done in earth, as it is in
heaven* (Mt. 6 : 10)?

When attempting to bring this teaching right through into
present-day life, one is confronted with an important problem.
The 'years of fire', through which mankind is passing, are offering men a great opportunity to follow the king of love. Many
clever and astute arguments are put forward by the materialist,
which people find themselves unable to answer. We recognise the
difficulties that have to be faced in what are called practical
politics. Many a deeply-read student already knows truth, even as
Pilate knew it, but like Pilate, when he comes to put truth into
practice he lacks the courage. The Master understood the difficulties, and understands them today, but still would have you try
to put into practice the law of Christ in every detail of your life.

As an example, in the Garden of Gethsemane, Jesus cried to
his Father: *O my Father, if it be possible, let this cup pass from me:
nevertheless not as I will, but as thou wilt* (Mt. 26 : 39). Or, as St
John has it: *the cup which my Father hath given me, shall I not
drink it?* (18:11). Every soul at some time has to face this tremendous issue, and either yield itself, or refuse to surrender to the
will of God. Nor is the issue always clear-cut. It is not a question
of saying, 'it is God's will that these terrible things should happen' and making no effort to help yourself, and still less to relieve
pain and suffering in others. To look upon all ills as inevitable is
not true surrender to the will of God; for God created a beautiful
world and created man and endowed him with the gift of His

Son, to enjoy his life, to be happy. Nevertheless, man's soul will be called upon to undergo certain experiences which we will call initiation. Preparation for initiation is sometimes unpalatable – it may take the form of bereavement, of the surrender of a loved one; or of a big change in life from which the soul shrinks simply because it clings to the familiar and objects to going forward into the unknown. A struggle with itself follows which causes pain. If only the soul could understand and know that God is all love, and that the experiences which come are to initiate him, to open the way to greater glory; and if it could then say, without bitterness or resentment, 'not my will, but thine, be done', (Lk. 22:42) then so much suffering would be transmuted. This is divine submission (not sacrifice, for sacrifice is something different) in accordance with the law of love. Jesus, knowing that a certain path had to be trod, went quietly forward to meet that which was appointed.

Let us picture Jesus in the Garden of Gethsemane with his disciples, including Judas. You will remember we likened the lower aspect of man's nature to the Judas-aspect, the aspect which betrays us, the baser self of man. Judas it was who led the soldiers towards Jesus . . . who kissed him . . . who betrayed him. The disciples around Jesus, particularly Peter, grew indignant when the soldiers dared to lay hands upon their beloved Master. Peter did what was natural and in accordance with his lower nature, and with a sword struck the ear of a soldier. By that same act he broke the law of love. Jesus, recognising this, said instantly, *Put up thy sword into the sheath.* (Jn. 18:11). Then by a supreme act of compassion Jesus healed the wound (Lk. 22:51).

This brings up a very terrible problem. Many are confused today by the violence and warfare. 'Is it right to fight, is it right to defend ourselves?' they say. The question becomes acute in time of war. Do you remember how the Master answered a similar problem by saying, *Render therefore unto Caesar the things which are Caesar's; and unto God the things that are God's* (Mt. 22:21)? Then people say: 'But if we refuse to fight we shall certainly perish; that cannot be right. Surely there is such a thing as righteous indignation, a righteous war?' We accept that attitude of mind, but what we are trying to stress is the meaning of this eighteenth chapter, that Christ's kingdom is the kingdom of love, and that throughout life if you would live in Christ's kingdom and be his disciple, you must live in accordance with the law of love. Love is the supreme power in the universe. God is love; and only when love is withdrawn from any situation can conflict, war and death ensue.

We have heard it argued that in certain circumstances there is nothing left to do except to fight. From the material point of view this may be right, but from the spiritual, never. Conflict is always, *always* a violation of the law of Christ. There is only one way to receive love into human life, and that is to give forth love. When there is violation of the law of love, suffering, conflict and pain will result.*

Peter obviously had not understood the Master's teaching, or he would never have raised his sword. Some will say at this, 'But you can't stand by and see an innocent man led to his death without doing something!' We agree that this is a difficult problem. Yet the power of love is supreme; and if this power is projected from the soul it will prove itself the stronger. We mean by this that if an innocent man were attacked, the power of a love flowing, shall we say, from a brother or a master of the light could protect that man. The world will not believe or accept this statement, but we make it without reservation.

When Peter broke the law of love he also shattered the light and the protection gathered around the Master and the disciples; and then the Master Jesus was arrested and the disciples scattered. Peter, following the crowd, went into the hall of justice and stood there warming himself by the fire. One of the maidservants standing by spoke to him. *Art not thou also one of this man's disciples?* (Jn. 18 : 17). This was a direct challenge and opportunity to Peter to stand forth and declare himself. Peter denied his Master.

Later Pilate questioned Jesus, asking him who he was. By the

* See Appendix, p. 189, 'Warfare'.

nature of his questions it can be seen that Pilate recognised Jesus as a true man even while he accused him. Jesus, knowing that Peter was standing near, answered Pilate by saying *Ask them which heard me, what I have said unto them* (21). In other words he was appealing to Peter to stand up and testify of that which he had heard and seen. And again Peter denied knowledge of Christ.

Cannot you see this happening today? There is no moral courage in the heart of men and women to speak out and testify to spiritual truth. Notice that the Master offered Peter another opportunity, but Peter did not respond and so broke the law a second time. Love and truth are the expression of the life of the spirit, of the power of Christ. Once the law is broken the life is broken and the power is gone. With spiritual law it is necessary to be consistent and so let it work out to its logical conclusion.

(18:1–6) *When Jesus had spoken these words, he went forth with his disciples over the brook Cedron, where was a garden into the which he entered, and his disciples. And Judas also, which betrayed him, knew the place: for Jesus ofttimes resorted thither with his disciples. Judas then, having received a band of men and officers from the chief priests and Pharisees, cometh thither with lanterns and torches and weapons. Jesus therefore, knowing all things that should come upon him, went forth, and said unto them, Whom seek ye? They answered him, Jesus of Nazareth. Jesus saith unto them, I am he. And Judas also, which betrayed him, stood with them. As soon then as he had said unto them, I am he, they went backward, and fell to the ground.*

Jesus asked the soldiers, *Whom seek ye?* When they answered, knowing what was in their minds he replied, *I am he.* Jesus was thus surrendering himself, submitting to the law. Yet notice that in accordance with the law of love the soldiers fell back – they could not lay hands upon him because Jesus was still protected. By saying, *I am he*, Jesus was further strengthening or building around himself the protection of the white light. Peter's raising of the sword against a fellow creature shattered it.

(18:7–11) *Then asked he them again, Whom seek ye? And they*

said, Jesus of Nazareth. Jesus answered, I have told you that I am
he: if therefore ye seek me, let these go their way: That the saying
might be fulfilled, which he spake, Of them which thou gavest me
have I lost none. Then Simon Peter having a sword drew it, and
smote the high priest's servant, and cut off his right ear. The
servant's name was Malchus. Then said Jesus unto Peter, Put up thy
sword into the sheath: the cup which my Father hath given me, shall
I not drink it?

Shall I not drink it? . . . the act of surrender. Jesus did not
desire Peter or anyone else to enter into conflict on his behalf. He
accepted the cup, knowing there was a way he had to follow.
Here is the lesson – to accept without resentment what cannot be
avoided, for it is your karma. Such an acceptance is a great test, a
great mystery. The wise and the initiated always surrender to the
will of the divine. By the word surrender we mean that when you
are confronted with an unalterable condition, it is obviously your
karma and you must not fight it. Do not kick against the pricks.
Accept what comes with tranquillity, knowing that it is the will
of God and that its purpose is the ultimate happiness and perfecting of the human soul.

(18 : 12–40) Then the band and the captain and officers of the
Jews took Jesus, and bound him, and led him away to Annas first;
for he was father in law to Caiaphas, which was the high priest that
same year. Now Caiaphas was he, which gave counsel to the Jews,
that it was expedient that one man should die for the people.

And Simon Peter followed Jesus, and so did another disciple;
that disciple was known unto the high priest and went in with Jesus
into the palace of the high priest. But Peter stood at the door with-
out. Then went out that other disciple, which was known unto the
high priest, and spake unto her that kept the door, and brought in
Peter. Then saith the damsel that kept the door unto Peter, Art not
thou also one of this man's disciples? He saith, I am not. And the
servants and officers stood there who had made a fire of coals; for it
was cold: and they warmed themselves: and Peter stood with them,
and warmed himself.

The high priest then asked Jesus of his disciples, and of his doctrine. Jesus answered him, I spake openly to the world; I ever taught in the synagogue, and in the temple, whither the Jews always resort; and in secret have I said nothing. Why askest thou me? ask them which heard me, what I have said unto them: behold, they know what I said.

And when he had thus spoken, one of the officers which stood by struck Jesus with the palm of his hand, saying, Answerest thou the high priest so?

Jesus answered him, If I have spoken evil, bear witness of the evil: but if well, why smitest thou me?

Now Annas had sent him bound unto Caiaphas the high priest. And Simon Peter stood and warmed himself. They said therefore unto him, Art not thou also one of his disciples? He denied it, and said, I am not. One of the servants of the high priest, being his kinsman whose ear Peter cut off, saith, Did not I see thee in the garden with him? Peter then denied again: and immediately the cock crew.

Then led they Jesus from Caiaphas unto the hall of judgment: and it was early; and they themseves went not into the judgment hall, lest they should be defiled; but that they might eat the passover. Pilate then went out unto them and said, What accusation bring ye against this man? They answered and said unto him, If he were not a malefactor, we would not have delivered him up unto thee.

Then said Pilate unto them, Take ye him, and judge him according to your law.

The Jews therefore said unto him, It is not lawful for us to put any man to death: That the saying of Jesus might be fulfilled which he spake, signifying what death he should die.

Then Pilate entered into the judgment hall again, and called Jesus, and said unto him, Art thou the King of the Jews?

Jesus answered him, Sayest thou this thing of thyself, or did others tell it thee of me?

Pilate answered, Am I a Jew? Thine own nation and the chief priests have delivered thee unto me: what hast thou done?

Jesus answered, My kingdom is not of this world: if my kingdom were of this world, then would my servants fight, that I should not be delivered to the Jews: but now is my kingdom not from hence.

Pilate therefore said unto him, Art thou a king then?

Jesus answered, Thou sayest that I am a king. To this end was I born, and for this cause came I into the world, that I should bear witness unto the truth. Every one that is of the truth heareth my voice.

Pilate saith unto him, What is truth? And when he had said this, he went out again unto the Jews, and saith unto them, I find in him no fault at all. But ye have a custom, that I should release unto you one at the passover: will ye therefore that I release unto you the King of the Jews? Then cried they all again, saying, Not this man, but Barabbas. Now Barabbas was a robber.

Everyone who allows the truth within to rule, who allows truth to vibrate through his being, hears the voice of his master and is a king of truth. Jesus is trying to teach a simple lesson to which we turn a deaf ear and a blind eye. The law of life is love. The law of the kingdom of heaven is love, and the kingdom of heaven is the kingdom of truth. Those who would enter the kingdom must be faithful to the law of love, to the truth in themselves. As another wise one has said, 'To thine own self be true'. Every master of spiritual law teaches us to be true to the law of spirit, to the law of God. Do not allow any tempter to deflect you from the path of truth, but have the moral courage to remain true to yourself.

To us it seems that there can be no compromise with truth, yet the world is continually making such a compromise. People will say that you cannot always be loving or forgiving. This is because they are not seeing with clear vision. The two paths are unmistakably outlined by the writer of this chapter – the path of the spiritual man, the true disciple of Christ; and that of the worshipper of Mammon, the follower of materialism. Once the disciple is accepted, at all times and in every circumstance he remains true to spiritual law as it has been revealed to him.

The Nineteenth Chapter

THE BLOOMING OF THE ROSE

A ROSE is called the flower of love and often used as a token of love. The human heart, like the rose, can turn towards the Sun, towards the blessing of the light; and, receiving, can expand in wisdom and understanding. There is so much behind and within the teaching of Jesus that only the heart can understand. For two thousand years men have been seeking understanding on the mental plane, at the mental level, but seeking largely in vain. There have been those, however, who have not only read the ancient scripts but who have entered the inner sanctuary to meditate and absorb the light. There they have found truth; but truth can only really be found when the heart is selfless at the time of meditation; and when it so aspires that the outer life also becomes selfless, with thought only for the needs of others. In such a one the rose starts to bloom and shed its fragrance through the life. Centuries after, the world acclaims such people as saints, as elder brethren, as masters.

A master is one who has attained mastery over the lower self, and on every plane of being. Such mastery arises from strength of spirit, which is love. Love is the power by which a master works his white magic. The greatest power in this world or the next is love, and love is power, love is wisdom. Wisdom, love and power are inseparable – three in one and one in three. Love is the link which binds and yet gives complete freedom; when applied it never fails, no matter how difficult a problem confronts the soul. When in doubt, fear, anxiety, in sickness, or when death draws near, the key to freedom, the key to heaven itself, is love towards God.

In the chapter to which we shall now turn – the nineteenth chapter – this truth is superbly demonstrated. We remind you that the mission of Jesus when on earth was to reveal the law in

162

action. You may remember the example of the overwhelming love of the Master for Judas his betrayer. Jesus, knowing that Judas through his karma was destined to betray him, drew that karma to himself, aware that he (Jesus) would forgive Judas and thus release him from the bondage. *Greater love hath no man ...* (15:13).

This chapter recounts two more occasions where Jesus deliberately set himself to release someone from the karma which must result from following a certain course of action. Thus is brotherhood demonstrated – how, by exerting a silent loving influence and by kind and selfless action, a man can save another from incurring karma of great suffering. Thus we find Jesus trying to draw out the good in Pontius Pilate, giving him opportunities to respond to his higher self and do the right thing. However, Pilate proved himself morally weak and could not grasp his opportunity.

We would also draw your attention to an episode when Jesus, according to John, *that the scripture might be fulfilled, saith, I thirst* (28). He knew that before him stood a soldier whose karma was about to give him an opportunity to be compassionate, to do a kind action, and the soldier, touched with pity, filled a sponge with vinegar and raised the sponge to the Master's lips. Then said Jesus *It is finished* (30), meaning that he had blest and helped the last soul on earth whom he could help in this manner, to transmute his karma.

There had been Judas, Pilate, and lastly this soldier. There had been many, many others. The truth is that the whole ministry of the Master was one of compassion, with regard not only to the bodily life but to the souls of those whom he came to succour.

Then follows the incident where the soldier thrust a sword into the side of Jesus and blood and water gushed forth, which is yet another symbol of the wonderful surrender of Jesus to the supreme love of God. Not only did he surrender his physical life, but he also gave in fulness his psyche. Few people, either in life or in death are able to make this final and supreme surrender

163

to God. Most pass over retaining earthly or astral desires. This is natural and will happen until the soul is so spiritually illumined that it can surrender all. Through this symbol of the blood and the water Jesus demonstrated that he had yielded himself body and soul to the love of God (water being symbolic of the soul or psyche) as a final demonstration to his followers and to all aspiring souls that the crown of life is utter surrender to God.

When you read this chapter, bear in mind that it describes in symbolic form the experiences every soul must undergo, in its own degree, while striving to follow the spiritual path. The soul, in its stand for truth, is mocked and scourged by the world, and by the worldliness within itself, and much that it holds sacred is trampled underfoot. The story of Jesus is the story of every aspiring brother, every disciple on the path.

(19:1–4) *Then Pilate therefore took Jesus and scourged him. And the soldiers plaited a crown of thorns, and put it on his head, and they put on him a purple robe, and said, Hail, King of the Jews! and they smote him with their hands. Pilate therefore went forth again, and saith unto them, Behold, I bring him forth to you, that he may know that I find no fault in him.*

You will notice that Pilate was capable of recognising the truth in Jesus, but was weak in himself. Pilate provides an apt example of the reaction of the worldly mind or the young soul which, seeing truth, lacks resolution and confidence to put truth into action. Because Jesus was aware that Pilate could recognise truth, he tried to help Pilate to be morally strong, as you will see.

(19:5–11) *Then came Jesus forth, wearing the crown of thorns, and the purple robe. And Pilate saith unto them, Behold the man! When the chief priests therefore and officers saw him, they cried out, saying, Crucify him, crucify him.*

Pilate saith unto them, Take ye him, and crucify him: for I find no fault in him.

The Jews answered him, We have a law, and by our law he ought to die, because he made himself the Son of God.

When Pilate therefore heard that saying, he was the more afraid; and went again into the judgment hall, and saith unto Jesus, Whence art thou? But Jesus gave him no answer. Then saith Pilate unto him, Speakest thou not unto me? knowest thou not that I have power to crucify thee, and have power to release thee?

Jesus answered, Thou couldest have no power at all against me, except it were given thee from above: therefore he that delivered me unto thee hath the greater sin.

As we have said, love is the greatest power on earth, the greatest power in heaven. Jesus possessed the power of love, real love, in his heart. He knew that love was the law of the universe, supreme over all, so he could say with tranquillity, 'you have no power to hurt me'. Here is the great truth we all have to grasp; for when love reigns supreme and radiates from the heart there is nothing on earth or in the planes beyond which can hurt the soul. If a man acts from the heart of love towards God and his brother he has nothing to fear, no matter how adverse his circumstances. If a man lives by love, all will come right in the end. Love is supreme over all. Do your best, act from the heart of love (which means putting into practice the divine law in your life), and you may have confidence in God that all will be well.

When Jesus said, *he that delivered me unto thee hath the greater sin* (11), he was showing compassion to Pilate, showing sympathy and understanding that Pilate had been placed in this predicament against his will; again by his compassion Jesus was offering Pilate an opportunity to respond to his higher self and make a stand for truth.

(19:12–15) *And from thenceforth Pilate sought to release him: but the Jews cried out, saying, If thou let this man go, thou art not Caesar's friend: whosoever maketh himself a king speaketh against Caesar. When Pilate therefore heard that saying, he brought Jesus forth, and sat down in the judgment seat in a place that is called the Pavement, but in the Hebrew, Gabbatha. And it was the preparation of the passover, and about the sixth hour: and he saith unto the Jews, Behold your King! But they cried out, Away with him, away*

with him, crucify him. Pilate saith unto them, Shall I crucify your
King? The chief priests answered, We have no king but Caesar.

Again we see the way of the world. The chief priests would
acknowledge none but the worldly king. They knew no king but
Caesar, the king of this world. In this manner the world denies
and crucifies the men of God. How vital it is for those on the
spiritual path to learn to look beneath the surface and into the
heart of another, to recognise the spirit, to see the best and to try
to understand the motive behind the action of another and not
merely assume it to be unkind. We should endeavour to see into
the heart with compassion and understanding, even of him who
appears to be our enemy. All brothers of the light should aspire
to act from the heart of love, which is truth. If we could only
remember that men's motives may be good even if their acts
seem to deny that goodness, it would save us so much suffering
and pain. Look ever, brethren, for spiritual kings; and when you
recognise them, do not crucify them by ingratitude or spite.

(19:16–18) *Then delivered he him therefore unto them to be cru-*
cified. And they took Jesus, and led him away. And he bearing his
cross went forth into a place called the place of a skull, which is
called in the Hebrew Golgotha: Where they crucified him, and two
other with him, on either side one, and Jesus in the midst.

This is interesting. They took Jesus to the place of the skull,
and there crucified him. A skull suggests to us a vacant head –
empty, hollow, unseeing, unknowing, without animation or perception. You see the esoteric significance? It means that it was
from a level of consciousness which was simply devoid of
understanding, all knowledge, all love, all beauty that they crucified the Son of God. It is happening still. At a place (or level)
where understanding is dead and the mind empty of pity, souls
are still crucified. Well might Jesus pray, *Father, forgive them;*
for they know not what they do (Lk. 23:34). For they who did
this deed were as skulls – empty, sightless, unknowing.

(19:19–42) *And Pilate wrote a title and put it on the cross. And the writing was,* JESUS OF NAZARETH THE KING OF THE JEWS. *This title then read many of the Jews: for the place where Jesus was crucified was nigh to the city: and it was written in Hebrew, and Greek, and Latin. Then said the chief priests of the Jews to Pilate, Write not, the King of the Jews: but that he said, I am King of the Jews.*

Pilate answered, What I have written I have written.

Then the soldiers, when they had crucified Jesus, took his garments, and made four parts, to every soldier a part; and also his coat: now the coat was without seam, woven from the top throughout. They said therefore among themselves, Let us not rend it, but cast lots for it, whose it shall be: that the scriptures might be fulfilled, which saith, They parted my raiment among them, and for my vesture they did cast lots. These things therefore the soldiers did.

Now there stood by the cross of Jesus his mother, and his mother's sister, Mary the wife of Cleophas, and Mary Magdalene. When Jesus therefore saw his mother, and the disciple standing by, whom he loved, he saith unto his mother, Woman, behold thy son! Then saith he to the disciple, Behold thy mother! And from that hour that disciple took her unto his own home. After this, Jesus knowing that all things were now accomplished, that the scripture might be fulfilled, saith, I thirst. Now there was set a vessel full of vinegar: and they filled a sponge with vinegar, and put it upon hyssop, and put it to his mouth. When Jesus therefore had received the vinegar, he said, It is finished: and he bowed his head, and gave up the ghost. The Jews therefore, because it was the preparation, that the bodies should not remain upon the cross on the sabbath day (for that sabbath day was an high day), besought Pilate that their legs might be broken, and that they might be taken away. Then came the soldiers, and brake the legs of the first, and of the other which was crucified with him. But when they came to Jesus, and saw that he was dead already, they brake not his legs: but one of the soldiers with a spear pierced his side, and forthwith came there out blood and water.

And he that saw it bare record, and his record is true: and he knoweth that he saith true, that ye might believe. For these things were done, that the scripture should be fulfilled, A bone of him shall not be broken. And again another scripture saith, They shall look on him whom they pierced.

And after this Joseph of Arimathaea, being a disciple of Jesus, but secretly for fear of the Jews, besought Pilate that he might take away the body of Jesus: and Pilate gave him leave. He came therefore, and took the body of Jesus. And there came also Nicodemus, which at the first came to Jesus by night, and brought a mixture of myrrh and aloes, about an hundred pound weight. Then took they the body of Jesus, and wound it in linen clothes with the spices, as the manner of the Jews is to bury. Now in the place where he was crucified there was a garden; and in the garden a new sepulchre, wherein was never man yet laid. There laid they Jesus therefore because of the Jews' preparation day; for the sepulchre was nigh at hand.

We would add that when Jesus called to the disciple to behold his mother and to his mother to behold her son, his words can be interpreted as a renunciation of human relationships for the term of that incarnation. To every soul when it departs from the body will come a like moment of renunciation. Only one relationship is eternal and that is on the spiritual plane, a relationship which is of the spirit. Jesus clearly demonstrated the necessity for renunciation of all worldly possessions even to the distribution of his garments.

Throughout his life it is clear that Jesus had insight into the akashic records, into the karma of those whom he contacted. We can see many examples of this foreknowledge of the exact working out of karma, which Jesus clearly and profoundly understood. His whole ministry was directed towards helping others either to transmute their karma or to work it out in a higher or better way. Upon all who have a deeper knowledge of the divine laws rests a like responsibility – to help those they meet not to make additional hard karma, but rather create good karma for the blessing and happiness of all mankind in the future.

How important it is for men of today to understand this law, for as surely as night follows day, what is sown today is reaped tomorrow; nations making bad karma will duly suffer both individually and nationally. It does not matter what others do. What we do is vital. Live the gospel of the brotherhood of man, live the divine law of love, and watch with what precision the law of karma, which governs the whole of man's life in this world and the next, will operate.

O Father Mother God, make clean our hearts within us so that we may see the vision of the true life which Thou wouldst have us live. May we be filled with the light of the Christ spirit and dwell in peace with our brother. Thus may we know Thy peace, always. Amen.

The Twentieth Chapter

'TOUCH ME NOT; FOR I AM NOT YET ASCENDED TO MY FATHER'

(20 : 1–31) THE FIRST *day of the week cometh Mary Magdalene early, when it was yet dark, unto the sepulchre, and seeth the stone taken away from the sepulchre. Then she runneth, and cometh to Simon Peter, and to the other disciple, whom Jesus loved, and saith unto them, They have taken away the Lord out of the sepulchre, and we know not where they have laid him. Peter therefore went forth, and that other disciple, and came to the sepulchre. So they ran both together: and the other disciple did outrun Peter, and came first to the sepulchre. And he stooping down, and looking in, saw the linen clothes lying; yet went he not in. Then cometh Simon Peter following him, and went into the sepulchre, and seeth the linen clothes lie, and the napkin, that was about his head, not lying with the linen clothes, but wrapped together in a place by itself. Then went in also that other disciple, which came first to the sepulchre, and he saw, and believed. For as yet they knew not the scripture, that he must rise again from the dead. Then the disciples went away again unto their own home.*

But Mary stood without at the sepulchre weeping: and as she wept, she stooped down, and looked into the sepulchre, and seeth two angels in white sitting, the one at the head, and the other at the feet, where the body of Jesus had lain. And they say unto her, Woman, why weepest thou?

She saith unto them, Because they have taken away my Lord, and I know not where they have laid him. And when she had thus said, she turned herself back, and saw Jesus standing, and knew not that it was Jesus.

Jesus saith unto her, Woman, why weepest thou? whom seekest thou?

She, supposing him to be the gardener, saith unto him, Sir, if thou have borne him hence, tell me where thou hast laid him, and I will take him away.

Jesus saith unto her, Mary.

She turned herself, and saith unto him, Rabboni; which is to say, Master.

Jesus saith unto her, Touch me not; for I am not yet ascended to my Father: but go to my brethren, and say unto them, I ascend unto my Father, and your Father; and to my God, and your God.

Mary Magdalene came and told the disciples that she had seen the Lord, and that he had spoken these things unto her. Then the same day at evening, being the first day of the week, when the doors were shut where the disciples were assembled for fear of the Jews, came Jesus and stood in the midst, and saith unto them, Peace be unto you. And when he had so said, he shewed unto them his hands and his side. Then were the disciples glad, when they saw the Lord. Then said Jesus to them again, Peace be unto you: as my Father hath sent me, even so send I you. And when he had said this, he breathed on them, and saith unto them, Receive ye the Holy Ghost: Whose soever sins ye remit, they are remitted unto them; and whose soever sins ye retain, they are retained.

But Thomas, one of the twelve, called Didymus, was not with them when Jesus came. The other disciples therefore said unto him, We have seen the Lord. But he said unto them, Except I shall see in his hands the print of the nails, and put my finger into the print of the nails, and thrust my hand into his side, I will not believe. And after eight days again his disciples were within, and Thomas with them: then came Jesus, the doors being shut, and stood in the midst, and said, Peace be unto you.

Then saith he to Thomas, Reach hither thy finger, and behold my hands; and reach hither thy hand, and thrust it into my side: and be not faithless, but believing.

And Thomas answered and said unto him, My Lord and my God.

Jesus saith unto him, Thomas, because thou hast seen me, thou hast believed: blessed are they that have not seen, and yet have believed.

And many other signs truly did Jesus in the presence of his dis-

ciples, which are not written in this book: But these are written,
that ye might believe that Jesus is the Christ, the Son of God; and
that believing ye might have life through his name.

In the age that is passing the gospels have largely been interpreted from the mental and emotional level; but we are now
entering the Age of Aquarius, when understanding will be from
the spirit. Once men open their hearts to the spirit, they will
understand the spiritual meaning of the gospels. The first essential towards such an understanding is for the soul to surrender to God's love. It is a temptation to insist upon reason being
satisfied before such a surrender of the soul to the light of Christ
within, or the voice of Christ, which is intuition, can take place;
but we dare to say that it is better to be guided by intuition, by
pure innermost feeling, than to succumb to the tempter, the
lower mind, or 'cold reason' which can tempt the soul away
from heavenly truth or divine intelligence. Truth is so simple,
and yet people rush hither and thither seeking sensation instead
of turning to their own true self for truth. Within, my brother, is
the altar of Christ. Kneel in all sincerity and humility and wait –
if necessary all your life; but kneel before that inner altar in
surrender to God, and there find truth.

This same 'cold reason' has always brought controversy about
the resurrection. According to the gospels the actual physical
body of the Master was raised from the dead. Was it not this
same body that entered the upper room? Did not Thomas
thrust his finger into the nail-prints on the Master's hands and
into his side, which had been pierced by the spear of the soldier? How could any other but a physical body return bearing
these scars? Where did the physical body disappear to if it had
not risen from the grave? There were the grave-clothes carefully folded and laid aside – a detail symbolical, of course, of the
man who had finished with earthly raiment, or with that clothing
of the soul beneath which many people become so smothered
that they cannot breathe the purer air of the spiritual spheres.
Their materialism weighs them down.

It is interesting that it was a woman, the womanly, the gentle feminine aspect of man's soul, which was the first to seek the Christ, the first to recognise the radiant presence. In other words, it is the loving, tender, gentle – the so-called feminine attributes – in either man or woman which will first behold the Lord. This was truly a spiritual manifestation, but it was something else, for did he not say, *Touch me not; for I am not yet ascended to my Father* (17). From which we think that it was the psyche or psychic body in which he appeared (not a materialised or ectoplasmic body as is sometimes suggested); a psychic body which was yet waiting to be interpenetrated by the perfect and pure spiritual atoms which alone can make that psyche eternal.

The astral or psychic body is temporal in nature until it becomes purified and given eternal life by undergoing the second death, when it is then reborn into the eternal kingdom of God. So the Master said, *Touch me not; for I am not yet ascended to my Father*. He did not desire contact with any mortal, or material vibration at that moment. Later he appeared in the upper room. If this was his physical body, how did he enter through a closed door? We are aware that a psychic and occult law exists which enables a physical object to pass through matter, so will not say that it is impossible, but we suggest that on this occasion the psyche of the Master appeared. He reappeared later to Thomas and later still to other disciples on the road to Emmaus, as we have read in the gospel.

If we agree that these were appearances of the psychic body, what had happened to the physical? We think that the body of Jesus had become so pure that it had disintegrated; that is, all that was mortal had returned to the elements. The rest was transmuted, become spiritualised, and formed part of the arisen body of Jesus.

We want you to understand that the story of the crucifixion and resurrection of Jesus was more than a symbol of life after death. It was an actual happening by which Jesus demonstrated that the man of God, living a life of purity, holiness and joy, gained the power over physical matter. He proved that by living the life of God, the soul gains command of physical atoms and physical life.

Life on earth is not meant to destroy men but to give them life, fresh life, more glorious life. The very atoms of the physical body were purified and transmuted from the matter of earth to the higher ethers, but Jesus was still visible and still audible to those around him. We can assure you that there is no truth at all in the fairy tale that his enemies took his body away and hid it. Jesus rose in all his joy and thanksgiving to his Father Mother God. The atoms of the physical form were spiritualised, transmuted to a higher ether. We say this without any equivocation. Jesus demonstrated to all men the truth that life never ceases, that man has within him the divine spark which, through many incarnations, is gradually growing, expanding and penetrating and controlling all the physical atoms.

There comes a time when the solar or Christ-power so interpenetrates the physical body that its earthiness gradually falls away, gradually dies – dust to dust, ashes to ashes. These words refer not just to the disintegration of a physical body that you know and love, but the gradual falling away of those atoms which are of the earth, earthy. But there are spiritual atoms which at the same time are entering the physical body and gradually recreating it and making it a body of light, a true solar body which, instead of being subject to disease and decay, has entered into eternal life. 'I will give you eternal life!' This is the real meaning of what Jesus said, and is the truth of all time. Man's body will be revivified, recreated, glorified by the Solar Logos. Thus there will be no more death, no more wailing and gnashing of teeth, no more sorrow because man will have entered into the full glory of his being, that which was intended for him when the world began; man will have entered into the promised land.

We suggest that in the ultimate the body of the perfected man will be laid aside when it is finished with and will vanish. It will not decay because no evil will remain to cause it to decay. It will return to the elements.

Our last point is one which has aroused much controversy. It is to do with those verses which declare that Jesus gave his disciples authority to remit sins, and from which the Church has assumed that its priests have power to remit the sins of penitents.

Then said Jesus to them again, Peace be unto you: as my Father hath sent me, even so send I you. And when he had said this, he breathed on them, and saith unto them, Receive ye the Holy Ghost; whose soever sins ye remit, they are remitted unto them; and whose soever sins ye retain, they are retained (21–23). Jesus breathed on them. In other words he instilled into the disciples spiritual light, life, truth. He caused them to absorb from him the magic of divine love. Divine love in any soul can give that soul power to remit sins or karmic debts, in this way only. The law of karma governs human life, and should you retain vengeance against someone who has injured you, you are chained to that brother's sins; it will remain a karmic debt through the ages because (like a ball) the debt travels backwards and forwards between you. If another person injures you and you are angry, unconsciously you retain a desire for vengeance in your soul. You may forget it in time, but it still binds you together. When you reincarnate you will meet again. Possibly you will pay back your debt by injuring that soul because in a past incarnation it once injured you. This is how karmic law works – backwards and forwards, backwards and forwards. I hit you, you hit me – so it goes on perhaps through many lives; and whilst that continues two souls are chained together.

The only way by which such a sin can be remitted or erased is for one of the parties concerned to forgive his enemy. Throughout this gospel we find that the Master Jesus had the power to look into a man's karma, and see the debts he owed to others and those debts which were owing to him. To one person after another did he offer an opportunity to erase such karma. Although Judas injured the Master, he forgave Judas, so drawing Judas's karma to himself. Again, the last words uttered by Jesus on the cross were, *Father, forgive them; for they know not what they do* (Lk. 23:34).

This is the secret of the remission of sins. Jesus *breathed on them*, or the Christ spirit instilled divine love into the heart, a love which caused the recipient to forgive his enemies. Thus does the Christ spirit cleanse the soul of sin.

Be thankful and live to serve your brother and to breathe upon him the divine love of the Christ within your heart.

The Twenty-First Chapter

THE LIFE OF SERVICE

IT IS not only in the words we speak, but in the response that quickens in you as you listen to or read our words, that you will find truth. We would like you, too, to feel the intermingling between the worlds, between man and the world of spirit, to become aware of angelic beings who pour cosmic rays upon you, as you aspire to heaven and to truth, quickening the vibrations of your soul, and the inner light. We in the world of spirit come back to earth to guide and encourage our brethren, and there are some on earth still attached to the physical body who can rise to planes of spirit to help those newly released from earth. Thus there is a beautiful intermingling between the earth and the spirit world, an interpenetration of life and service. We love to serve, for how can we enjoy heaven whilst loved ones on earth still need our help? We serve because we love. This is our happiness.

Let us now read the twenty-first chapter of the gospel and seek an inner interpretation of it.

(21:1–25) *After these things Jesus shewed himself again to the disciples at the sea of Tiberias; and on this wise shewed he himself. There were together Simon Peter, and Thomas called Didymus, and Nathanael of Cana in Galilee, and the sons of Zebedee, and two other of his disciples. Simon Peter saith unto them, I go a fishing. They say unto him, We also go with thee. They went forth, and entered into a ship immediately; and that night they caught nothing. But when the morning was now come, Jesus stood on the shore: but the disciples knew not that it was Jesus.*

Then Jesus saith unto them, Children, have ye any meat? They answered him, No. And he said unto them, Cast the net on the right side of the ship, and ye shall find. They cast therefore, and now they were not able to draw it for the multitude of fishes. Therefore that disciple whom Jesus loved saith unto Peter, It is the Lord. Now when Simon Peter heard that it was the Lord, he girt his fisher's coat unto him (for he was naked), and did cast himself into the sea. And the other disciples came in a little ship (for they were not far from land, but as it were two hundred cubits), dragging the net with fishes. As soon then as they were come to land, they saw a fire of coals there, and fish laid thereon, and bread.

Jesus saith unto them, Bring of the fish which ye have now caught. Simon Peter went up, and drew the net to land full of great fishes, an hundred and fifty and three: and for all there were so many, yet was not the net broken. Jesus saith unto them, Come and dine.

And none of the disciples durst ask him, Who art thou? knowing that it was the Lord. Jesus then cometh, and taketh bread, and giveth them, and fish likewise.

This is now the third time that Jesus shewed himself to his disciples, after that he was risen from the dead. So when they had dined, Jesus saith to Simon Peter, Simon, son of Jonas, lovest thou me more than these?

He saith unto him, Yea, Lord; thou knowest that I love thee.

He saith unto him, Feed my lambs. He saith to him again the second time, Simon, son of Jonas, lovest thou me?

He saith unto him, Yea, Lord; thou knowest that I love thee.

He saith unto him, Feed my sheep. He saith unto him the third time, Simon, son of Jonas, lovest thou me?

Peter was grieved because he said unto him the third time, Lovest thou me? And he said unto him, Lord, thou knowest all things; thou knowest that I love thee. Jesus saith unto him, Feed my sheep. Verily, verily, I say unto thee, When thou wast young, thou girdedst thyself, and walkedst whither thou wouldest: but when thou shalt be old, thou shalt stretch forth thy hands, and another shall gird thee, and carry thee whither thou wouldest not. This spake he, signifying by what death he should glorify God. And when he had spoken this, he saith unto him, Follow me.

Then Peter, turning about, seeth the disciple whom Jesus loved following; which also leaned on his breast at supper, and said, Lord, which is he that betrayeth thee? Peter seeing him saith to Jesus, Lord, and what shall this man do?

Jesus saith unto him, If I will that he tarry till I come, what is that to thee? follow thou me.

Then went this saying abroad among the brethren, that that disciple should not die: yet Jesus said not unto him, He shall not die: but, If I will that he tarry till I come, what is that to thee?

This is the disciple which testifieth of these things, and wrote these things: and we know that his testimony is true. And there are also many other things which Jesus did, the which, if they should be written every one, I suppose that even the world itself could not contain the books that should be written. Amen.

Throughout his ministry, the Master continually made use of the symbol of the bread and the fish.

We hope we have made it clear that the resurrection of the body of Jesus did in a sense take place; but that its elements had become so purified by the Christ light and love which had manifested through them that nothing remained to cause decay, as in ordinary death. It was the true body of the arisen Christ which manifested to the disciples.

Remember, they had undergone a terrible ordeal; they had seen their Lord taken and crucified, and it seemed that with all his glory and greatness he could not save himself from his enemies, so the disciples were heart-broken and disillusioned.

In spite of all Jesus had taught them, they were still wrapped up in their personal selves, conscious mainly of their physical needs. So when their Master was slain they lost faith, they were back where they had started, with their attention centred on practical things such as a means of livelihood. So often it happens that souls are raised to a state of spiritual ecstasy and then some trouble comes along and faith and belief are shattered, and the heavens seem as brass. It is a major test of their steadfastness and sincerity which they cannot pass. They say, 'I trusted, believed, and thought I was following the Master and it did not work, and now everything has gone wrong! I will have nothing more to do with religion'.

This is exactly how the disciples were feeling; and so they put to sea to get on with earning their living, unaware that their Master was with them all the time, and that what they really needed was spiritual food. Before, he had been continually sustaining their spirit; now they were left – just as you will be left at some time, just as you will stand alone when your testing comes. What then? Will you follow the spirit or will you return to worldliness?

The sea, the water, is always the symbol of the soul. The fish is symbolic of spiritual food. The Master knew exactly what the disciples needed. In his great love he manifested to them yet again to lead them to the food they so sorely needed. And when he was recognised, standing on the shore, Peter impulsively jumped into the water, so ardently did he desire to reach his Master.

You will notice that Jesus asked the same question of Peter three times. As Peter had denied him thrice Jesus tested him thrice. *Lovest thou me more than these?* he asked. *Thou knowest that I love thee* (15). But Jesus was aware Peter had yet to realise what love meant. Possibly Peter knew all about love in his mind, but had yet to absorb the Christ love into his being. This so often happens; people know all the esoteric truths with their minds, and yet because they cannot *feel* love, because they do not know what it means to love, they cannot recognise truth. To love means to surrender all to God in a complete giving, an outpouring of the whole being.

Jesus bade them cast the net on the right side of the boat – in other words, saying, 'Seek your spiritual food in the right way'. If you work solely for the welfare of the body you will catch nothing; if you seek purely intellectually you will be disappointed. But if you cast your net on the right side in the right way your net will be filled to breaking point with all the sustenance you need, yet the net will not break.

Then follows an interesting point. We are told that the Master had kindled a fire to cook the fishes. As the story is told by John it seems natural enough; the Master was there waiting to receive his friends, having lit a fire wherewith to cook the fish. But do you not understand that this was a spiritual fire, a divine fire which Christ kindled on behalf of his disciples? In other words he quickened within them the divine fire of love. When their hearts were thus opened, when once the divine fire burned within, then they were ready to receive the food so divinely prepared and made ready for them. Then at last their soul-hunger was satisfied.

After having undergone such an experience, such a revelation, to live for themselves and for their own material comfort and satisfaction could no longer content the disciples, for at last they knew what they needed. Those who abandon the spiritual path because they feel deserted, because they become disillusioned, will forever experience the same yearning spiritual hunger. They must come back again, they cannot help coming back. *Lovest thou me? Yea, Lord; thou knowest that I love thee. Feed my lambs . . . Feed my sheep* (15–17). Three times the Master asked Peter, so that, when the time came, Peter would not waver.

And then Peter sees the beloved disciple following Jesus and asks, *and what shall this man do?* (21). Why did Peter speak in this manner? Jesus answered him, *what is that to thee?* It sounds simple enough; but the inner meaning to us all is this. Jesus says to us in effect, 'Get on with your own work. What your brother disciple has to do does not concern you'.

This at first sight seems difficult to understand, because on the other hand we are told to bear our brother's burden, to help our brother, and to be concerned about his welfare.

Yet the two injunctions can be balanced simply and easily. They mean that while we are to take a sympathetic interest in our brother's welfare, we may not pry into his intimate affairs. While ready to help him should he call upon us, we may not try to limit him. He has to go his way, under command of the great lords of karma. *If I will that he tarry till I come, what is that to thee?* (22). We must not judge another, he has his task to fulfil.

There is another, deeper, interpretation to which we would draw your attention. We suggest that when Jesus said *If I will that he tarry till I come, what is that to thee?* he was showing that John is not only the man, but is the representative of the soul, tarrying on earth until the divine life, the light, the Son, comes and gathers its beloved from the darkness. The souls which cannot respond to the divine fire when it comes, must wait until the light comes again in a new cycle.

We come to bring you what knowledge we can to help you to purify the soul-body. Do not be content to drift as life takes you. Work continually for the purification of the soul-body. Respond to that light which shines in you; which urges you to purity of thought and life, to kindliness and love, to knowledge of the higher worlds, and wisdom in the soul.

The church of St Peter was built upon the earth, was built for the mind of the body, as on a rock. The mind can understand the teachings of the church of St Peter. But that which is to come in the new age, the Aquarian Age, the age of brotherhood, is the church of St John, who represents the soul, the psyche, when the soul and body will be illumined, transmuted by Christ the Son.

The gospel of St John contains the mystical teachings of all the ages, in rather veiled outline but clear to the initiated. It sets out a code of conduct which the initiated cannot help but follow. It is not a question of 'You must be good . . . you must love your brother man', but rather that when illumination comes there is only one way in which it is possible to live, and that is by spontaneous love, kindness, gentleness, not only to brother man but to our lesser brethren the animals, and indeed to all created things.

The whole life and ministry of Jesus as told by St John is the symbolical story of man's life on earth, his spiritual unfoldment and, if you like to use the word, redemption. Every man is the Jesus-man. In every man and woman and child is the divine spark, the life; and the spiritual life-blood of the man is the Son, the Christ. In man's journey through life he has to learn the one supreme truth of life, that within himself are the two aspects; the material or the earthly aspect on the one hand, the man part; and on the other, the Christ, the spiritual aspect. Everyone sooner or later has to learn that lesson which is indicated by the shedding of the blood, *the blood of Jesus Christ his Son cleanseth us from all sin* (1 Jn. 1:7). It is not physical blood. It is the shedding of the spiritual heart's blood. As the soul toils in the darkness of earth, as the soul is striving and struggling to rise into spiritual freedom, the man is sorrowing because there is ever this pull, this tug-of-war between the higher and the lower self.

'Drink', the Master said, 'Take this cup and drink in remembrance of me'. What does this mean, my brethren? That you should take and drink the cup of human life and human experience, however bitter it may be. Accept it. Learn your lesson of acceptance; for as you take the cup and drink, remembering the Christ in you, your acceptance means that you are being redeemed by the spirit of Christ that is within. Say, 'In the name of Christ, the supreme light, the perfect Son of God, I accept my karma; I drink the cup and the life-forces of the Christ fill my whole being and my past errors are washed away'. Why does this cleansing take place? Because with the accepting of the cup, the vision is cleared and the soul sees its past error, and having realised it, experienced it, it is finished.

Karma is a law of God, a cosmic law which cannot be altered. But when the soul has passed through the experience of what you like to call evil or bad karma, the soul has had its opportunity to pay a debt, remit its sin. The soul can only remit its sin by accepting its own guilt. It is not (as we have formerly supposed) the fact that the Master Jesus was crucified that has redeemed us from our sins. It is the fact that we ourselves in physical life are being crucified by our karma; and because the lower self is purified by the higher self or the Christ self, past sins are washed away.

We speak as one of you. We *are* one of you, my brethren, because we suffer as you suffer. Love gives us understanding, it makes us feel for you, to feel as you feel. We feel for you, we understand you, we absorb from you your heartaches. But your sorrows do not weigh us down, because love is the divine transmuter. Love, as you have learned, is the alchemist which transmutes the base metal of earthliness, the pain and the passions of earth. Love transmutes all this, absorbs it into itself, changes it into pure gold.

When we say we suffer with you it is because we identify ourselves with your experiences; but we absorb from you and transmute the experience. This is why you feel strengthened after contact with your teacher, and you know that all is well; in meditation and communion he has brought the light and the love of God which reigns supreme in the heavenly state, and you are uplifted and strengthened and blessed by it. But you have to learn yourself to receive the cup and transmute the sorrows and sufferings of your earthly life. The Christ in you has to transmute and redeem you; then the lower self passes away and has power over you no longer. Jesus the Christ upon the cross demonstrated this cosmic truth to all the world. The crucifixion spells the surrender of the man to God, the heavenly Father. Remember this, whatever you are enduring at the present time. It may be a minor crucifixion but it is actually the salvation of your soul; your higher self will draw much closer as a result of the remission of your particular sin.

This is a truth which all initiates learn. No matter what their religion or their belief, all will come face to face with this opportunity of reaching upwards. The divine power of love will be their saviour.

We would draw your attention again to the betrayal of Jesus by Judas. Again, Judas dwells in every man. Within us all is the Judas which betrays our Lord. But Jesus, who might have felt much resentment, forgave Judas and pitied him. He loved him. He drew upon himself the karma of Judas because he could forgive Judas and give him love which wiped out the karma.

On other occasions we have said that to keep up a feud or a quarrel, no matter whether within your own family or in the larger family which is the outside world, or between nations, can only end in one way – destruction. This is the vital lesson which the world today must learn. We know the many arguments that will leap to your mind – how impossible it is, for instance, for one nation to forgive another – or even for one individual who has a righteous claim against another to feel forgiveness. But, my brethren, it is a cosmic law which no soul, no country can escape. There must be forgiveness because without it the soul cannot be redeemed. Without forgiveness the sins of the individual cannot be washed away; but when the person or nation will drink the cup, accept, admit the fault, then man or nation will be saved and released from the karma that binds it.

May the keynote of all thought and action be gentleness and love. This is the meaning of the remission of sins through the Lord Christ, the light, the Son of the creator, the Father Mother. When this truth is understood men will become once more united with God, and the holy Trinity, Father Mother Son, will be complete. The light shall shine down on the earth and man shall reach upward to the heaven; and the perfect form of the six-pointed star, the basis of all creation, will be once more manifesting in all its glory on earth. Then man's incarnations will cease and he will pass onward into spheres of more glorious life and joy.

O God, may the world be hastened on its path of spiritual evolution and come speedily into the new and golden day of happiness, beauty and love which Thou hast ordained for man, Thy son.

APPENDIX

[THESE notes are passages from White Eagle's teaching, much of it subsequent to the original messages, and which amplify one or two particular points in the main commentary. It was felt that they were of greater length than the demands of the narrative would permit, but that readers might still find in them something of use.]

BAPTISM (*Chapter 1, p. 7, refers*)

As with all ceremonies, the esoteric meaning of baptism has been lost, associated as it has become with the idea that children born into this physical world are born in sin, and therefore that entry into Christ's kingdom is denied until they are baptized, washed clean of that same original sin which brought them to birth. This conception arose and has persisted from a misreading of the story of the fall of man – a wonderful symbolical story now brought almost to ridicule by the analysis of the earthly mind of man.

But let us go deeper than this. When the soul passes away at death it carries with it a certain residue, even after purification by passage through the purgatorial spheres; this residue – we may call it the seed-atom if you like – is incorporated again when the new vehicle is built for the next life on earth. So there are transmitted to the newly-born soul certain characteristics, urges and desires which play an important part in the coming life on earth. These desires and urges can be helped, purified and cleansed by the raising of the inner vehicles – those subtler bodies now incarnated in the physical.

The ceremony of baptism marks an important epoch in growth and evolution. Jesus set the example. John the Baptist was the forerunner, a high initiate sent forth to prepare the way for the coming of the bearer of the light of the world. John's mission was to call the people to baptism, to be cleansed, to receive the power of the Holy Ghost. It seems clear that the Master Jesus fully understood John's mission; for he himself, before starting his ministry, was baptized by John – an important point to remember, because Jesus was destined to turn the arc of evolution upward. And the baptism itself emphasised a profound inner truth, as shown by the tremendous power which came upon the Master, the symbol of the dove descending upon him, and the voice crying, *This is my beloved Son, in whom I am well pleased* (Mt. 3:17).

At that moment the physical body and all the subtler bodies of the Master Jesus received contact with what is known as the Holy Ghost. It meant no other than union of Man with God.

JUDGMENT (*Chapter 5, p. 45, and Chapter 8, p. 67, refer*)

It is said that in the world of spirit all is made plain and clear. Now on earth you look as through a dark glass which distorts the soul of man, but when you are released from the body you see face to face, and you see yourself as in a mirror. This is the true judgment. In the old days orthodoxy taught you that you would stand before a judge who would condemn you to hell or raise you to heaven. This is the old orthodox Christian teaching. But may we show you what really happens to a man in spirit when he leaves the body and all earthly things? He is very tenderly cared for. He is not judged, nor is he condemned. He is taken in due course into the temple of the Holy Grail, and all around the walls of that temple are mirrors. The man is bidden to look into that mirror, and he sees moving pictures of himself and of his life on earth. He sees himself as he truly is. No one judges him; he judges himself, because he sees clearly, with sorrow and thankfulness, what he is and how he has behaved in his life on

187

earth. This is the judgment, this is the moment of choice between heaven or hell; because if this soul accepts in humility the lesson so beautifully shown to him, he sees not only the dark self but also he sees his heavenly self, his true self, and he reaches towards his true, his heavenly self. He goes to heaven not only because he sees the good in himself, but he sees the good in all his companions. But if he rejects the truth which is being shown him, he himself chooses the darkness which is on the astral plane, where his soul goes for a time.

MIND (*Chapter 10, p. 88, refers*)

[In all the discussion of the way into the sheepfold, White Eagle seems to be distinguishing between the true way, the way of love, and the way of the mind, the 'destroyer of the real'. Elsewhere he has said,]

The mind is eager all the time to reason out and test everything which is said. There are, however, many things which the eager physical brain can never comprehend because in itself it is not an efficient instrument. Man needs something more than intellect if he would understand the mysteries.

The man of brilliant intellect must find himself at a dead end, when he can make no further progress unless he also has a child-like heart, and can come back to the beginning and start as a little child, simple and trusting.

Man is so interested in words. He enjoys mental stimulation and interest but soon he forgets. Only in the deep silence, in meditation and contemplation before the throne of God does man grow towards God. It is in meditation and contemplation of the qualities of the divine Father and Mother that he evolves towards the divine Parent, in spirit, in spiritual stature until he becomes at last the perfect son of God.

Man has lost so much through Western materialism. He has lost his soul of truth with the development of his mental body. Through too much mental activity the heart-mind or the heart-body is neglected until sorrow or physical pain and suffering come. Then the powerful and greedy intellect cannot supply any-thing which will assuage pain or comfort the sad and the lonely. One thing only can support man in his hour of need. This is the light which shines from the mountain top down into man's heart, and carries with it a truth which opens his eyes; so that he learns of the place to which he is journeying. This brings hope and even joy to the man of sorrow. The little seed, the precious jewel within the lotus of the heart quickens and grows. This is why we continually say that meditation is of the utmost importance if you wish to unfold the true light. Books are all very well; studying comparative religions can be helpful, mental gymnastics can be exciting, but they cannot give you what this inner light can give. Nevertheless, we agree that development of the intellect, if in-spired and guided by that inner light, will lead to greater powers of comprehension and a quickening of intelligence. But we repeat that it is essential for a soul to look up and aspire; in other words, to strive to unfold the seed or light within, which is the true light of God.

This has been called the still small voice of conscience. People neglect it. They are too busy. If they read their scriptures they would know that whenever a man of God sought communion with God, sought inspiration from God, he went up into a moun-tain. Moses when called by God ascended Mount Sinai, and there received the Commandments. Jesus went up into a moun-tain and when he was set his disciples came, and he opened his mouth and taught them. All masters first of all raise the con-sciousness of their pupils. Pupils cannot remain on the level of earth; they rise into a higher state of consciousness. Only at that higher level can heavenly truth be received. You can only attune yourself if you are above the earth.

WARFARE (*Chapter 18, p. 157, refers, and also Chapter 3, p. 21*)

[The eighteenth chapter of the gospel tells how Peter drew a sword and wounded one of the soldiers who came to arrest Jesus in the Garden of Gethsemane. The comment that follows is that had not Peter thus broken the law of love by recourse to arms, or by an act of retaliation, the spiritual powers surrounding Jesus would have sufficed to protect both him and the disciples. The teaching on St John's gospel was given during World War II, and the question naturally arose, 'What about all those young men who have been compelled to go to fight in self-defence and to defend others, are they then sinning by breaking the law of love?' And White Eagle's answer was:]

The men who went to fight did so in the main believing they were doing right. According to their understanding they made a sacrifice and will receive corresponding blessing. But this does not alter the spiritual law of love and brotherhood. The soul can sacrifice itself even if mistaken. In each instance it is offered an opportunity to have its eyes opened and so better understand spiritual law. This law, however, remains; man must love his brother.

Life has become chaotic because man in the first place descended from the heights and broke the law of love, thereby creating for himself a collective or world karma, a karma in which all share and must face up to at some time or another. As a result the world as a whole, the soul of the world, will learn and men will no longer be confronted with a situation in which it would seem they can do no other than fight. There are individual cases even now where men and women seem to be lifted out of the conflict, so that they are not called upon to fight – this again is the result of their own karma. There can be no injustice in the law which is outworking through each individual life. No one can interfere with the outworking of karmic law, but we of the spirit labour incessantly to heal the wounds which follow, to bring peace, light and comfort to our brothers. Individually, the souls of these men and women caught up in battle receive recompense and blessing in accordance with their degree of sacrifice and the motive impelling them.

Against this people will remind us that Jesus said, *Greater love hath no man than this, that a man lay down his life for his friends* (Jn. 15 : 13). True, those words express the law of love; and when man gives himself selflessly to what he thinks is the law of love, his giving is truly sacrificial and he receives the blessing. But Jesus did not mean merely a surrender of mortal life, but the supreme renunciation of self so that others may receive good. These truths must be interpreted on the spiritual plane. Materialisation of spiritual truth is a mistake continually being made. Even the orthodox church tends to try to fit everything into some material concept. We must seek spiritual understanding so that we live from the spirit and recognise that life is based upon spiritual values before we can enter the kingdom of happiness.

SUBJECT INDEX

193

INDEX